The Positive Psychology of Buddhism and Yoga

Paths to a Mature Happiness

With a Special Application to Handling Anger

For Nelson Burack
With best wishes –
Mar Levine

The Positive Psychology
of
Buddhism and Yoga

Paths to a Mature Happiness

With a Special Application to Handling Anger

Marvin Levine
State University of New York at Stony Brook

 LAWRENCE ERLBAUM ASSOCIATES, PUBLISHERS
2000   Mahwah, New Jersey   London

Portions of this text have been taken from Levine, Marvin, EFFECTIVE PROBLEM SOLVING, 2/e ©1994, pp. 96–112. Reprinted by permission of Prentice Hall, Upper Saddle River, New Jersey.

Lawrence Erlbaum Associates, Inc., Publishers
10 Industrial Avenue
Mahwah, NJ 07430

Cover design by Kathryn Houghtaling Lacey

Library of Congress Cataloging-in-Publication Data

Levine, Marvin, 1928-
   The positive psychology of Buddhism and yoga : paths to mature happiness / Marvin Levine.
          p. cm.
   Includes bibliographical references and index.
   ISBN 0-8058-3349-8 (cloth: alk. Paper)
ISBN 0-8058-3833-3 (pbk.: alk. paper)
   1. Buddhism—Psychology.   2. Yoga—Psychology.   3. Spiritual life—Psychology. 4. Maturation (Psychology)—Religious aspects. 5. Self-actualization (Psychology)   I. Title.
   BQ4570.P76+   2000
   294.3'01'9—dc21   00-022894
                                                                  CIP

Books published by Lawrence Erlbaum Associates are printed on acid-free paper, and their bindings are chosen for strength and durability.

Printed in the United States of America
10 9 8 7 6 5 4 3 2

*This book is dedicated to those
who long ago abandoned their childhood beliefs
and are still trying to fill the emptiness.*

Contents

Part I: Buddhism

Part III: Extended Supplements

Table of Anecdotes and Tales

Foreword

This book begins with questions: What is maturity? What do we mean when we say "He made a mature decision"? What is the relation between maturity and serenity? How do we attain these conditions? The principal thesis of this book is that Buddhism and Yoga provide answers to these questions. Essentially, the teachings first reveal the pitfalls in ordinary, unreflective living. They then provide guidelines and practices for transforming ourselves, for progressing to a new mode of living. This transformation is accomplished by taming the cravings (passions, fears, agitations) and by challenging conditioned beliefs (attitudes, habits of thought). When transformed, we are more than mature; we face the hurly-burly of the world with wisdom, hardiness, and confidence.

Within Western psychology a movement has appeared recently by the name *positive psychology*. It focuses on transforming ordinary living into a richer, more enhanced, more mature happiness. Buddhism and Yoga are the quintessential positive psychologies. Indeed, they provide the intellectual framework for such a psychology.

A secondary thesis of this book is that the outlook of Western psychology is congenial with that of Buddhism and Yoga. The aspects of Western psychology that are complementary to Buddhism and Yoga are brought out in essays at the end of relevant chapters. Parts 3 and 4 of this volume demonstrate more completely this dovetailing of Eastern and Western psychology.

Introduction

This book has a special form. Before I describe it, let me first tell you about myself, and how I came to write it. I was born Jewish and, until I was 10, was educated in Orthodox Judaism. The vision I absorbed, a monotheistic God surrounded by angels who painted sunsets and watched out for me, was of a warm and friendly universe. Like many American Jewish youths, however, I grew away from Judaism in my teens. But that vision, that cosmology, persisted, although I wasn't aware of it. Awareness came at Columbia University starting with a freshman humanities course, where I was immersed in the literature and culture of ancient Greece. For the first time I saw another culture, dazzling in its creative and intellectual activity, that had a totally different cosmology. I asked a classmate "How could the Greeks, who were so advanced, be so naive as to believe in many Gods?" My friend's answer was simple and irrefutable: "Maybe they were right." I stammered indignantly, but knew that I had no real defense of my childhood beliefs. My subsequent education at Columbia was heavily influenced by the cultural-relativistic outlook of its distinguished Anthropology Department, and by the strong environmentalism of its psychology program. Students were confronted with the challenge that their beliefs and values were arbitrary, conditioned by their culture and their upbringing. Where previously I had a home base, an island in a world of flux, now I was cast adrift.

Two enduring products of my Columbia education were that I started studying psychology, eventually developing a career as a research psychologist, and I became a spiritual seeker, reading philosophy and religious literature. I knew little of Eastern writings until, in my mid-20s, I read Sir Edwin Arnold's *The Light of Asia* (1894). This was a poetic rendering of the life of Siddhartha Gautama, later called the Buddha, of whom I had known nothing. I was particularly impressed with the totality of Siddhartha's renunciation. He left his home, yes, but it was no ordinary home. This was not a slave in material misery turning away to find happiness in some other realm. Siddhartha was a prince with every talent, pleasure, and promise a human being can have. But this was not good enough. All of it was renounced. The symbolism was intriguing.

And so I started reading more Buddhist and then Hindu literature (the Buddha was Indian; his teachings reflect Hindu ideas). I described myself as a work-a-day psychologist and a weekend orientalist. Between this latter study, the later pursuit of Yoga, and my deepening understanding of the aims of clinical psychology, the ground started to form again beneath my feet. I was now in a position to envision a new cosmology, one that acknowledged the impact of cultural relativism and conditioning but went beyond it. The Buddha, incidentally, understood very well the arbitrariness of our belief systems. He saw this not as a cause of despair but as a challenge, one that he brilliantly overcomes.

In the meantime, my career had developed successfully. For 30 years I have been a faculty member at the State University of New York at Stony Brook, and a researcher in their Experimental Psychology Program. Some 20 years ago, one of my colleagues who knew of my interests in what I called Buddhist Psychology, asked me to present a lecture to the graduate students in the Clinical Psychology Program. I gave a 2-hour presentation that I entitled "Buddhism and Behaviorism." For a few years this was an annual event and earned me a local reputation as a psychologist interested in Eastern ideas.

Five years ago, after I was professor emeritus, a couple of the graduate students approached me, requesting more extensive presentations. I agreed to a series of weekly meetings on Buddhism and Yoga on the condition that a minimum of six people would regularly attend. We advertised among all (approximately 100) psychology graduate students and 20 people came! The weekly series ran through two semesters. In each of the years that followed, I again canvassed the students and even more signed on. My audience began to broaden. Faculty and nonuniversity people began attending. The director of The Round Table, a program for learning in retirement, heard of these presentations and invited me to offer the series to a large group of retirees. There was clearly an interest in learning what a psychologist had to say about Buddhism and Yoga.

The interest was manifested not only in the number of people attending but also in the responsiveness of the audiences. In all my years of teaching standard courses in psychology, I always knew when the hour was over. Five minutes before the end, I would hear papers rustling, feet shuffling, and chairs shifting. In this series, however, I would look up at the clock and see, with a start, that we were 10 minutes past the hour. No one was moving. All eyes were on me; everyone was absorbed, wanting to hear more. I had to announce the conclusion of the meeting, and even then people stayed to question and discuss. The interest in this subject was unmistakable. I decided, therefore, to organize my presentations for wider consumption— to put this material into a book.

When so much literature exists on Buddhism and Yoga, why another book? Readers can surely learn about Buddhism and Yoga from many other sources. This book describes Buddhist–Yogic ideas in relation to those of contemporary Western psychology. As a result, Western readers will find these Eastern ideas less exotic and more congenial with what I call the Western scientific worldview. Of course, the fact that this book relates Buddhism and Yoga to modern psychology does not make it unique. There are already several books that attempt to do this. However, my sense of the existing literature is that it approaches the topic backward. Authors typically begin with a description of meditation and compare it to psychotherapy. But why do Buddhists meditate? What are they seeking? Readers are given answers like "enlightenment," "satori," "nirvana," words that are highfalutin' and vague. Or authors begin with concepts like "emptiness" and "egolessness." Without adequate foundation, however, all these words sound mystical and puzzling. In this book, these puzzles do not exist. I begin with the Buddhist view of the human psyche and of the human condition. This leads to the question of what psychological changes need to be made to improve that condition. This view is then compared to Western psychological views. It is only after this is completely understood that I move to discuss meditation, now justified as a means to a goal, as a method for producing a certain kind of psychological change. Advanced concepts are introduced in later chapters. Western readers will find that initially they are asked to take less on faith, and as the more esoteric practices and ideas are appropriately introduced, will be more comfortable in their understanding.

Concerning the style of the book, two background facts are relevant. First, this is not written as a scholarly book. As a career scientist, I know the requirements of scholarship: the documentation, the proper source citation, the accuracy of quotes. In my years of philosophical readings, however, I was determinedly after the wisdom of the thing. I wanted only to let the material have its impact on me and to think about it. Throughout decades of reading I had no other long-range intentions. Hence, I never took notes, made outlines, or recorded sources. I never envisioned a time when I would need such material. In giving lectures and in writing this book, I did not permit this lack to hinder me. And so I frequently present remembered readings—some of the Hindu or Buddhist anecdotes for example—without giving the sources. I don't know them.

The second fact related to style is that this book derives from a set of oral presentations. Even though in our weekly meetings I did most of the speaking, I never thought of these as "lectures," and referred to them instead as "presentations." Much of the material consists of anecdotes and stories, which I presented using the storyteller's art. By this I mean that I didn't read them to the class from books (even when I remembered the source) but rather conveyed them, as storytellers do, with my own artistic sense. The effective presentation of the idea came first. If here and there a detail was changed, that was less important. In telling of the life of the Buddha, for example, I did not merely excerpt Arnold's *The Light of Asia* (which is an artistic rendering in its own right) or copy the description from any other source. I presented it with my own sense of the dramatic. In so doing, I felt that I was communicating more effectively. I have carried this style over to this book. I have tried to make the material as interesting as I possibly can. To you who feel that this attitude, this rewriting of the work of artists and scholars is presumptuous, I can only respond that this is what storytellers traditionally do.

This style, of course, also does not meet scholarly standards. To my colleagues with such standards, I apologize. I hope that this will not prevent them from being open to the wisdom that I am trying to transmit.

The book is divided into four parts. The first part is on Buddhism. As I describe in the text, Buddhism arose within, and was heavily influenced by Hinduism. Hinduism, and the philosophy of Yoga that emerged from Hinduism, historically preceded Buddhism. Nevertheless, I begin with Buddhism. The Buddha so elegantly systematized the Hindu ideas that, in his framework, they are most easily understood. Buddhism, of course, contains a vast literature developed over some 2,500 years. I present here only the most basic teachings attributed to sermons by the Buddha, himself. Thus, the treatment is introductory. Concepts that emerge from later Buddhism (e.g., Nirodha and Sunyata) do not appear here. It is hoped that this introduction will stimulate readers to seek deeper contact. At the end of this book, I recommend some follow-up readings.

The second part deals with Yoga. As I just noted, Buddhism arose in the context of Hinduism, and Yoga is an outgrowth directly from that context. Buddhism and Yoga, therefore, have a close family resemblance. Where the Buddhist section emphasizes the ideas, the Yoga section presents in detail, some of the Eastern practices. Thus, the Yoga section can be read as a continuation of the preceding section. Of course, ideas that are unique to Yoga are also presented.

The third part, referred to as "Extended Supplements" describes some aims and practices in Western clinical psychology. My deep-seated conviction is that the intellectual framework of Buddhism and Yoga is congenial with what I call the Western scientific worldview, particularly with the view within Western psychology of both human nature and the human circumstance. This relation between East and West is, indeed, one of the theses of this book. Throughout the Buddhism and Yoga sections, at the end of the chapters, I have added what I call *supplements*. These are typically signaled by three asterisks. These supplements describe aspects of Western psychology that relate to the material in that chapter. There are, however, relevant developments in contemporary clinical psychology so extensive and so worthy of detailed treatment, that I have added this extended supplementary section. It continues the demonstration of how some of the methods of Western psychology coordinate well with Eastern ideas.

The fourth part is on handling anger. The central lesson of the first three sections is that one can improve one's life by changing one's self. This fourth section applies this lesson and the methods of the three preceding sections to this specific area, to handling one's own anger. This topic is not only important in its own right but can serve as a model for changing other facets of ourselves.

It is commonplace to refer to a book as a journey. This book describes a path and invites the reader to start making progress on that path.

ACKNOWLEDGMENTS

I am grateful to many people who influenced the writing of this book. My wife, Mara, first encouraged me to undertake the project, and patiently applied her substantial writing talents to editing the successive drafts; Sung-Bae Park, a colleague at Stony Brook and a Korean Buddhist practitioner, also encouraged me, suggesting that Western psychology was an excellent way for Buddhism to come to America; Fred Levine, a friend and colleague in psychology, continually challenged me with his insightful questions; my many students over the years frequently stimulated and corrected my thinking; and prepublication reviewers, recruited by the publisher, made several useful suggestions. The input of all these people have, I believe, greatly improved the book.

I thank the State University of New York at Stony Brook—particularly Drs. Katkin, Logue, Brener and Whitehurst—for providing the resources needed both to teach the material and to write this book. And I must include my secretary, Sandi Cohen, who was always cheerful and efficient, even under the pressure of deadlines. Deserving of special thanks is my editor, Anne Duffy, my production editor, Renata S. Butera, along with Larry Erlbaum and the staff of LEA for their continued enthusiasm and support.

—*Marvin Levine*

PART I

BUDDHISM

1

King Ashoka's Question: What Is Your Secret?

The following legend is told of King Ashoka, a powerful ruler in India at about 250 B.C.

A messenger, sent by the Master of the Royal Torture Chamber, informed the king of a remarkable event. A heretic, although being tortured, showed complete indifference to the pain. The king was immediately interested and went himself to witness this phenomenon. Inside the desolate room he saw, in a pot of vigorously boiling water, an old man. This gentleman was chatting affably with the servants who were attempting to make the flames even hotter. When the king recovered from his astonishment, he ordered that the man be released and escorted to the palace.

Later at the palace the king had an interview with the fellow, now dressed in the saffron robe of a Buddhist monk. King Ashoka began by asking, "What is your secret?"

According to the legend, the monk replied by telling the king about the Buddha and Buddhist teachings, how these liberated him from all suffering. King Ashoka then had the monk instruct him in these teachings. The king converted to Buddhism and made it the national religion. He himself changed from a despotic conqueror into a beneficent ruler.

2

Maturity and Serenity

Tibet, a country that was entirely Buddhist, was invaded in 1949 by the Chinese. They then began the forcible conversion of this land into a Marxist state. The Dalai Lama, the country's spiritual leader, and many of the Buddhist monks escaped into exile. Since then, the Dalai Lama has traveled tirelessly trying to persuade the United Nations and various governments to pressure the Chinese into leaving Tibet. In a television interview, a reporter asked the Dalai Lama; "Aren't you ever angry at the Chinese?" The Dalai Lama replied, "They stole my country. Why should I let them steal my mind?"

During another interview about Tibet the Dalai Lama said "The enemy can be very important. The enemy teaches you patience."

What do we mean by the term *maturity,* as in "He behaved in a mature way?" What do we mean by *serenity*? We associate these states with wisdom and peace of mind, and generally regard them as ideals to be attained. Yet no one teaches us how to attain them. What produces mature behavior and serenity? Are there particular experiences we need? Are there techniques that, if faithfully applied, will produce them? How

5

can one attain wisdom, peace, patience, and freedom from anger, even when one is in the midst of life's struggles?

As the stories of the Dalai Lama suggest, these questions are taken very seriously in the East. Buddhism and Yoga have striven for thousands of years not only to answer such questions but to develop techniques for attaining this maturity, this in-the-world serenity.

We begin our quest for this goal as they do in the East, at the opposite end: We begin by understanding psychological suffering, that is, the experience of suffering, and with knowing how such suffering may be minimized and even eliminated. This apparent detour, according to the Eastern view, is really the start of the path to the goal. Suffering will be discussed not merely theoretically but concretely, in terms of pain, distress, frustration, and so on, including its various flare-ups and chronic forms. The chief starting questions are: What is the nature of this suffering? What causes it? What alleviates and puts an end to it?

In an effort to answer these questions, Buddhist and Hindu concepts of human nature as they developed in India more than 2,000 years ago are reviewed. In addition, these conceptions are periodically compared to relevant Western psychological ideas, for I clearly perceive an affinity between these Eastern views and the Western scientific view of human nature.

At the outset, let us acknowledge a basic similarity. The Western system of psychotherapy, with its various theoretical underpinnings such as Behaviorism or Psychoanalysis, has as its fundamental concern the understanding and alleviating of psychological suffering. So, also, does Buddhism. The great questions of suffering—its nature, cause, and alleviation—have motivated into being the entire religion.

Given, then, two worldviews with the same concerns, we should not be surprised that they have some similarity or that they complement each other. As I review the Buddhist (and later the yogic) system I pause periodically to present some relevant Western conception or method. Typically, these are found at the end of appropriate chapters.

FOR REFLECTION AND DISCUSSION

1. In one form of the legend, described in chapter 1, when King Ashoka asks "What is your secret?" the monk first replies "What

do you mean? What secret?" Do you find that an odd response? What does it imply?

2. One meaning of *mature*, of course, is *older*. But another meaning is a compliment as when we say of a child, "He behaved in a mature way" or of an adult, "That was a mature decision." Using this second meaning, give a specific example of an adult person's action in some situation where you might compliment him using the word "mature." Now give a general definition of the word "mature" when used as a compliment.

3. Sometimes we use the word *immature* as a criticism ("You're behaving in an immature way!"). What is the meaning of "immature" when used as a criticism?

3

The Story of Siddhartha

Like Jesus and Mohammed, the Buddha is a historical figure around whom a religion arose. The following story of his life is commonly told.

About 2,600 years ago, the ruler of a small Indian state fathered a son whom he named Siddhartha Gautama. At his birth, it was prophesied that Prince Siddhartha would grow up to be either a great king or a great spiritual leader. Siddhartha's father was clear about his own desires: He wanted his son to be a great king. To this end, the king had his son brought up with definite restrictions. Siddhartha was to be trained in the warrior and governing arts. He was not to receive religious teachings or to know the hardships of life. The father even feared the effects upon Siddhartha of the poverty and misery that might be seen in the surrounding towns. Therefore, he restricted him to the palace grounds. Until he grew to adulthood, Siddhartha did not regard this as confinement, for the grounds extended for miles and included beautiful parks and streams. The most pleasurable entertainments and the friendship of noble children were all his, and he held the status as the king's heir. He thus flourished within these golden walls. When Siddhartha was a young man, his father at-

tached him further to the royal life by having him marry a beautiful princess. Not long after, they had a son.

Siddhartha, now in his 20s, was fully aware of the confined life
he had been living. He had simply obeyed his father and had
stayed within the palace grounds. Nevertheless, he finally per-
suaded his father that he, the prince, should view the lands and
people that he would one day rule. The king agreed and set a date
for Siddhartha's excursion to the nearby villages.

The king, however, took no chances. He sent word to the surrounding communities about the upcoming visit. He ordered
that a festive welcome was to be given to his son, that on that day
none but the young and healthy were to be seen in their finest,
most colorful dress. The old, the sick, and the dying were to be
hidden away.

For all his precautions, however, the king failed. The selected day
arrives. The prince leaves the palace in a chariot, escorted by
Channa, his charioteer. The people, vigorous and colorfully ar-
rayed, line the streets. Siddhartha is dazzled by the beauty and ad-
miration of the crowd. Suddenly, however, there appears a
half-naked man, covered with oozing sores, emaciated from illness, collapsed on the ground. Siddhartha stops the chariot and inquires of Channa what that might be. Is that a human being?
Channa replies that he is indeed a human, but that he is ill.
Siddhartha asks what it means to be so ill. Is this some sort of punishment? Channa replies that it is not. What has happened to him
could happen to any of us. "Even to me?" "Even to you, oh
prince."

They ride on through the youthful, cheering throng when a second momentous event occurs. There appears an ancient, de-
crepit man, wrinkled, eyes clouded over, hanging weakly onto a
staff. Again, Siddhartha inquires and again is informed that this
is indeed a human and that his condition will be the condition of
all of us who live for so many years.

A third event occurs soon after. In the midst of the festivities, a
funeral procession appears. Siddhartha, startled by the grey mo-

tionless corpse, is informed by Channa that this is death, that the life of every one of us will end in this way.

Siddhartha, troubled, decides to return to the palace. On the way back they pass a man simply dressed, carrying a bowl for begging. He is a forest hermit, a type of spiritual seeker common in India at that time. Nevertheless, he is a novel and puzzling apparition to Siddhartha. Channa explains that the man is one who has withdrawn from the world in order to better understand himself and the world. He follows a path of the spirit.

They reenter the palace, but these four events have transformed Siddhartha. He sees now the potential horrors lurking behind the glittering surface of palace life. He sees his own vulnerability to life's sorrows and the pain that must be in the world. Remembering the fourth event, the forest hermit, he decides after a few weeks to become one of these. One night, taking tender leave of his sleeping wife and child, and without telling his father, he leaves the palace. Returning to where he had seen the monk he gives away his expensive clothes, and enters the forest hoping to find kindred souls who might teach him.

Before continuing with the tale, let us note the symbolic significance of Siddhartha's transformation. One might think that renunciation of the world is appropriate only for people who have little and are wretched to start with. Siddhartha, by his action, tells us that is not so. Even princely pleasures cannot compensate for the pain caused by ignorance of life. If we lack understanding, the richest, most luxurious life is not good enough.

We also can make here a comparison between West and East. Psychotherapy in the West is concerned with specific types of suffering: depression, phobias, obsessions, and the like. Buddhism begins with the more general framework of suffering: that derived from illness, aging, and the constant threat of death. As will be seen when we consider the teachings of the mature Buddha, the concept of suffering will be enlarged to cover not only this general framework but the Western clinician's concerns as well as other kinds of pain.

In the forest, Siddhartha meets fellow-seekers. He also finds teachers with whom he studies but who leave him ultimately unsatisfied. He and five other seekers like himself go off together and decide to practice a radical asceticism, literally starving themselves.

One day, when he is alone, Siddhartha faints from hunger. He is found by a young woman who revives and feeds him. Siddhartha realizes that asceticism was not leading him to the answers that he seeks. If anything, by so weakening him, it became a hindrance. As he had earlier rejected the life of pleasure, he now rejects the ascetic life. He understands that he is looking for something between the two, what he will later call The Middle Way.

With this in mind, he enters upon a great meditation. He emerges from it transformed. Not only has he seen the heart of life, but he has formulated his insights as a doctrine. By this vision, this enlightenment, he realizes that he is now beyond the reach of the pain of life's horrors, and is suffused by a profound serenity. This transformation is seen even in his outward behavior, with the result that people, sensing his wisdom and serenity, soon start calling him the Buddha, which means the Enlightened (or Awakened) One.

As the Buddha, he returns to his five colleagues in the forest and begins his teaching. They, struck by his remarkable contentment and by the depth of his insights, give up asceticism and become his first disciples. Soon other teachers, leaders of large sects, are won over. They and many of their followers swell the ranks of this new movement. By the time the Buddha is about 40 years old, the movement, although relatively small, is firmly established in India.

The Buddha lived another 40 years, the revered leader of this new "religion." I put the word in quotes because, as will be seen, no assumptions, visions, or beliefs about deity are invoked. In fact, Buddhism today is sometimes referred to as the atheistic religion.

FOR REFLECTION AND DISCUSSION

1. What do you think of Siddhartha's renunciation and the implications that "Even princely pleasures cannot compensate for the pain caused by ignorance of life?"
2. Buddhism is sometimes referred to as an atheistic religion. Can it be called a religion if there is no belief in God? What other qualities might it have to justify calling it a religion?

4

The Hindu Context

Before we review the teachings of the Buddha, it will help us to know something of the intellectual and religious context in which he lived. At that time (app. 500 B.C.), northern India had certain religious and philosophical parallels to ancient Greece. (This is probably no coincidence. Some 4,000 years ago, the same people in the northern part of the globe drifted south, some toward Europe and Greece, and some toward India. Knowledge of the classical Greek language, I am told, is of great benefit in studying Sanskrit, the ancient Indian language.) In Greece, religion functioned on two levels. There was the pantheon of gods that was part of the popular religion, but there was also the abstract characterization of the world and of man's place in it, which the philosophers were developing. The disparity between the two Greek views of the divine was made painfully clear by the death of Socrates. He, who taught the importance of contemplating the sublime essences, was executed for leading the young away from their (the popular) religion. The same duality of religious beliefs existed at the same time in India. There was a pantheon of gods, with accompanying stories, symbols, rituals, and rules of worship. There was also, however, the more philosophical approach that saw deity in a more abstract form. It is this latter philosophical religion that gave rise to

15

the movement we call Yoga and that influenced the Buddha. By first reviewing certain basic ideas in this philosophical context, we gain a better understanding of the Buddha's teaching. This review also helps explain my strategy of drawing examples from both Buddhist and Hindu sources.

In the Hindu-philosophical view, the personalized gods are replaced by a universal spirit, referred to as Atman. Atman pervades everything: sun, planets, stones, trees, insects, monkeys, you, and me. Our spiritual goal is to discover this Atman within ourselves and thus to connect with the all-pervasive Atman. The Atman within is to be discovered in a deeper place than our cravings, fears, and agitations, deeper than such ordinary mind activity as brooding, daydreaming, and planning. The Atman could only be glimpsed when all this restless craving and mind activity is stilled. The mind is likened to a lake. When turbulent, it is opaque but, when calm, it is transparent. Yoga was founded on this conception of an all-pervasive, inner and outer Atman. The term *yoga* means "linking," and is usually interpreted to mean linking the inner Atman with the outer.

The next important concept concerns suffering. The early Indian philosophers saw the ubiquitousness of *Dukkha*. This is a term that modern writers have translated as "suffering" but, in discussing the Buddha's teachings, we learn that Dukkha has a broader meaning. For the Indian philosophers, all human beings and, indeed, all creatures with feelings, start out "caught" or "stuck" in this world of Dukkha. How one accounts for this fact and what one does about it, were, for these philosophers, major issues.

The final concepts that we need to present here are those of reincarnation and Karma. The view was held that the Atman within us, like the Western concept of soul, is eternal. At the death of the body, it is transferred to another bodily existence. This belief was unquestioningly held. It was as much taken for granted as, for example, our contemporary belief that we're surrounded by an invisible substance called air. We hear about it from our youngest childhood and never think to question it. Similarly, for the ancient Hindus, the belief in reincarnation was pervasive, like the very air, so to speak, they breathed.

A concept associated with reincarnation is Karma. Karma is what might be called a causal principle. Your actions and your sufferings are determined by events in your previous lives. A kind of cosmic bookkeeping takes place: the better you were in previous lives, the better your actions are in this life and the closer you can come to true happiness.

*   *   *

The causal force of Karma has a loose analogy with the Western concept of determinism. If a baby is born with a birth defect the ancient Hindus would attribute it to Karma; we attribute it to some defect in the genetic material received from the parents. Both are strongly causal hypotheses.

FOR REFLECTION AND DISCUSSION

1. The Greeks of 500 B.C.E. believed in many gods. At the same time the Hindus, on the other side of the world, believed in many gods. Do you think this was purely a coincidence? Or would there be a connection between the two? Explain.
2. What is the difference between the concepts of determinism (as you understand it) and Karma? Do you believe in determinism (physical, psychological, economic)? If you do, does the idea of human freedom have any meaning?

5

The Core of the Buddha's Teachings

Dukkha, Atman, Reincarnation, Karma; these formed the conceptual framework in the Buddha's world, the framework within which he formulated his doctrine.

The Buddha began his teaching with four foundation principles. These are of such importance that they have come down to us as the Four Noble Truths (Rahula, 1974).[1] They are the roots of Buddhism. Virtually everything that follows in the succeeding years—the Buddha's sermons, books written through the centuries, commentaries on earlier writings—can be regarded as flowering from these Four Noble Truths. We will present these here in outline, with an expanded description in the next few chapters.

The Four Noble Truths are as follows:

1. The Truth of Dukkha (Suffering): We are vulnerable to a multitude of suffering experiences such as hunger, pain, fear, loneliness, hatred, and so on.

---

[1] A description of the Four Noble Truths will be found in almost any introductory book on Buddhism. I cite Rahula out of respect, because of the influence his book has had on me.

2. The Truth of Tanha (Craving): We are vulnerable because of the way human nature is constituted. Specifically, we are a bundle of urges that push and pull from within. Urges, for example, to obtain food, drink, sexuality, companionship; to escape pain, boredom, irritation.

3. The Truth of Nirvana (Liberation from Dukkha): Our vulnerability can be ended. We can attain freedom from Dukkha. We do this by changing ourselves, by transforming our cravings. We can subdue these overpowering urges that push us now one way, now another.

4. The Truth of Magga (The Eight-Fold Path): Liberation from Dukkha is attained by the practice of eight disciplines. These disciplines entail the cultivation of

   1. Right Understanding
   2. Right Thoughts
   3. Right Speech
   4. Right Action
   5. Right Livelihood
   6. Right Mindfulness
   7. Right Effort
   8. Right Meditation

These, then, are the four axioms of the system. Each one needs to be explained in greater detail. The next few chapters will be devoted to this elaboration.

We should notice first, certain absences in the Four Noble Truths, concepts that are not included. First, there is no mention of Atman. Nirvana is attained not by communing with the Atman, but by "calming the lake," by eliminating the turmoil of the pushes and pulls that overwhelm us. In fact, the Buddha rejected the concept of Atman. He called his doctrine one of Anatman (without Atman). This earned Buddhism the epithet "The Atheistic Religion." His justification is that in a thorough analysis of himself, he finds only psychological properties—sensations, feelings, urges. Nothing else, nothing like an everlasting "soul" or Atman. The Buddha advises his disciples to investigate this for themselves, to introspect deeply and to see whether anything beyond psychological process can be detected.

This Anatman doctrine has implications that are discussed later. We may note here that the doctrine created some difficulties among the early Buddhists. In one way or another, (arguably) Atman-like ideas reappeared in later Buddhist writings.

The second concept omitted in the Four Noble Truths is reincarnation. Unlike his rejection of the Atman concept, however, the Buddha continued to accept the idea of reincarnation. Clearly, however, the Four Noble Truths, with their singular focus on suffering, do not require a belief in reincarnation. The Buddha's teachings are as relevant in cultures like our own, where reincarnation is not widely accepted, as in cultures where it is.

*   *   *

By abandoning the Atman concept, the Buddha produced a change in the Hindu outlook, making it more akin to the contemporary scientific worldview. The Buddha never invokes a deity-concept to explain the cause of Dukkha or, indeed, of anything in the universe. Explanation without recourse to the action of a deity is, of course, one of the hallmarks of contemporary science. It is pithily portrayed in the following anecdote:

At the start of the 19th century, the great French astronomer, LaPlace, presented to the Academie Francaise his theory of the development of the solar system. He described how, from internal explosions, the sun spewed forth matter that, under the influence of its own internal gravitational forces, compressed itself into the various planets. When the presentation was completed, Napoleon, who was in the audience, asked the first question. "Where" he asked "was God in all this?" "Sire," replied LaPlace, "I have no need of that hypothesis."

Scientific explanation has proceeded without "that hypothesis" before and since. The religious criticism against Darwin's theory of evolution was for just that reason, that it removed God from the explanation of the appearance of the various species. "That hypothesis" was not needed even to explain the appearance of human beings.

FOR REFLECTION AND DISCUSSION

1. What is your view of the question of Atman? Do you feel that there is some essence within yourself that will continue on after your death? If so, what form do you picture it taking? Heavenly? Earthly? In some other galaxy? Would it have memory of your present existence?

2. In the statement of the First Noble Truth of Dukkha, there is listed a few unpleasant mental states (hunger, pain, hatred). We could add "shame" and "boredom." How many more can you think of? Make a list of as many unpleasant states of mind, mild as well as excruciating, as you can think of. Do you begin to understand why Buddhism focuses on Dukkha?

3. Buddhism is sometimes referred to as the pessimistic religion. Why do you think this is the case? Buddhism is sometimes referred to as the optimistic religion. Why do you think this is the case? One author writes that Buddhism is neither pessimistic nor optimistic; it is realistic. How would you interpret that?

6

The Noble Truth of Dukkha (Suffering), Part 1: Suffering and Transitoriness

The Truth of Dukkha: We are vulnerable to a multitude of suffering experiences.

Although "suffering" is the usual translation for *Dukkha*, the term really has three aspects. First, it characterizes a world in which there is a great deal of unhappiness, ranging from abject pain, loneliness, anxiety, hunger, being with hateful people, and loss of those we love, to unpleasant states of feeling such as anger, disgust, tension, and boredom, to mild discomforts both chronic (e.g., "life is meaningless") and occasional (e.g., a headache). We see explosions of Dukkha in the Holocaust, wars, and natural disasters. But, we also see it flare up again and again in the daily commonplace of disappointments, frustrations, insults, and embarrassments.

Second, Dukkha includes the idea of change, perpetual flux, what the Buddha refers to as "transitoriness." Nothing in the world of Dukkha is permanent. Therefore, this implies that misery is always potential. When it is said that someone is "in the world of Dukkha," that person may not be suffering now. The potentiality for suffering, however, is always present. For example, suppose a man responded to the preceding paragraph by saying, "All this talk of suffering does-n't apply to me. I have a well-paying, interesting job, a happy marriage, and good health. I sleep soundly at night and wake up zestfully, raring to go."

The Buddhist thesis would be: All the good features the fellow just cited are subject to change. For example, the man's wife may one day stop loving him. Or he may wake up one morning realizing that he no longer loves her. And the loss of job, health, or stability is notoriously common. The conditions of our happiness are always subject to change. So long as we are in the world of Dukkha, there is no state that will permit us to "live happily ever after."

We see this sense of potentiality in the Buddha's own life. He was at the pinnacle of the princely life with all imaginable power and plea-sure at his fingertips. But it wasn't good enough. The potential for misery was palpable.

Transitoriness and potentiality are also seen in a story told by the Greek historian, Herodotus, writing in the 5th century B.C. Herodotus describes the rise of the Persian Empire, its conquest of Asia, and its wars with the Greek city-states. In the course of this epic, he tells a tale about Croesus, an incredibly wealthy ruler of the kingdom of Lydia, in Asia Minor (Herodotus, 1942).[1]

> Despite the enormous wealth and power of Croesus, his king-dom was successfully invaded and finally conquered by one of the Persian armies. Croesus himself was captured and was to be executed. The Persian commanding general decided to burn the king at the stake and to make a public spectacle of the execution. Croesus, brought in shackles, was tied to the stake. Straw was pushed around him in preparation for the fire. He looked heav-enward and cried out woefully "Solon, Solon."

---

[1] I relate this and other tales here as a storyteller rather than as a scholar. The quotes, therefore, are for verisimilitude rather than for historical accuracy. See the Introduction for my justification of this style.

As it happened, the Persian general was a student of religions. Failing, however, to recognize this name, he asked his aides nearby "To what God is he crying out?" When no one could answer, he had Croesus untied and brought before him. He commanded, "Tell us about this god, Solon, to whom you were just now calling out." Croesus replied that Solon was not a god but a man, an elder statesman from Athens, long respected in that land. Croesus then related the following experience.

"Many months ago when we were still at peace and the Persian trumpet was distant, Solon had visited me. I personally escorted him about my realm displaying its glories and the luxuries of my surroundings. Proudly, I said, 'Solon, you have lived a long life and have traveled widely. Who is the happiest man you've ever known?' In response, Solon described an Athenian who was prosperous and whose sons, by their prowess in battle, brought glory to his name. I asked 'Well, then, who is the second happiest man you know?' Solon described another in a far off island. I now asked him directly 'What about me?' Solon replied 'Ah, your majesty. We in Athens have a saying: Never judge a man's happiness until he has died.' "

"At that time, I dismissed the remark as quaint, but I see now what Solon was trying to tell me."

The general was so touched by the wisdom of this tale that, according to Herodotus, he freed Croesus and enlisted him as an advisor.

Now let us respond to the fellow, who earlier objected to the emphasis on suffering, who gave evidence for his own happiness. The Buddhist answer is: "You are fortunate, indeed. Enjoy this good fortune. Savor and relish it. But be like the man who, while enjoying excellent health, immunizes himself against the chance of a future disease. Be like the man who, though the days are now sunny, builds his house to weather the storms. You are happy. That is wonderful. But don't drift in your happiness. There is work to be done."

"What is the work?" you ask. Read on.

FOR REFLECTION AND DISCUSSION

1. "Never judge a man's happiness until he has died." Can your
   happiness be assessed right now? If so, what is the meaning of
   Solon's statement?
2. Define transitoriness. Give an example. We acknowledge transitoriness by immunizing ourselves against disease. Can you
   think of other ways that we acknowledge transitoriness? For the
   Buddhists, transitoriness is an essential character of existence.
   Why do you think they put such stress on that idea?

7

The Noble Truth of Dukkha, Part 2: Caught in the Causal Matrix

We have so far considered two of the three aspects of Dukkha. First, life inevitably entails a great deal of suffering. This ranges from the acute (produced by wars, famines, disease, etc.) to the common-place (feelings that frequently wash over us: grouchiness, fear, anger, boredom, depression, aches and pains, loneliness, etc.). Second, although suffering is frequently not experienced, it is always potential. The angel of suffering, so to speak, lurks about us even in the best of times.

The third aspect is perhaps the most subtle. There is a causal character throughout Hindu and Buddhist thinking. It is not uncommon to read metaphors like: "The person in this world of Dukkha is like a leaf blown by the wind." Or ". . . is like a cork bobbing in the ocean, pushed this way, now that, by the waves." We have already discussed the concept of Karma, which holds that our current suffering, circumstances, and actions are the consequences of past lives. This is nicely illustrated in a scene from a Japanese film.[1]

A powerful warlord had, in his youth, attained to this power by ruthlessly destroying any person or family that had blocked his ambitions. On the palace grounds lived now a young woman, a Buddhist devotee, who was a daughter from one of these vanquished families. One day the two stopped to converse. The warlord said to her, "I did terrible deeds in my youth and many people now hate me. But you are different. I had your parents killed and your brothers exiled. Yet, you never show hatred or ill-will toward me." The Buddhist replied "How can I hate you? You only did what your Karma made you do."

This story illustrates the causal character of Karma. However, we may look ahead, and note another feature in this exchange. When one has the determinative sense of another, this sense of that person's actions arising from a matrix of forces, then one does not experience hatred.

Another example of the matrix of forces in which action occurs is seen in the concept of universal interdependence. A contemporary Buddhist monk from Vietnam, Thich Nhat Hanh, has described Siddhartha Gautama's life and the subsequent history of the Buddha in a clear poetic form. Thich Nhat Hanh (1991, p. 115) describes one of Siddhartha's insights as he was coming to enlightenment:

He looked up at a pippala leaf imprinted against the blue sky, its tail blowing back and forth as if calling him. Looking deeply at the leaf, he saw clearly the presence of the sun and stars—without the sun, without light and warmth, the leaf could not exist. *This was like this, because that was like that* (italics added). He also saw in the leaf the presence of clouds—without clouds, there could be no rain, and without rain, the leaf could not be. He saw the earth, time, space, and mind—all were present in the leaf. In fact, at that very moment, the entire universe existed in that leaf.

This interdependence applies, of course, to all life, including each human life. Siddhartha's meditating where and when he did was de-

---

[1]This scene occurs in a Japanese film that I saw several years ago. While I vividly remember the scene I have been unable to remember or to locate the film itself. A similar exchange, however, occurs in the film *Ran* by Kurasawa.

pendent on the four signs (chap. 3) he had experienced on that fateful ride with Channa. All of us can see how our present circumstance exquisitely depends on prior events.

> I once had a friend who was relating the utter mismatch of his parents. Weary from hearing their perpetual squabbling, he intoned "They never should have married." I thought "And who would be standing here talking to me now?"

Note, incidentally, that the marriage of this couple, some 80 years ago in Russia, was affecting me then and is affecting you, the reader, right now.

There is, then, a sense of causality, of a matrix of forces, so long as we are in the world of Dukkha. In particular, our inner life is at the mercy of those forces. Someone insults us and we experience anger; someone cheats us and we brood for a day and a lose a night's sleep; we experience disgust, fear, frustration as a result of various events. Thus, our inner life is like a leaf blown by the wind.

The complete conception of Dukkha, then, is as follows: We are each of us caught in a matrix, a universe of forces that frequently produces our unhappiness. That unhappiness can range from the acute (inconsolable grief, desperate hunger, excruciating pain, etc.) to the commonplace (feeling blue, grouchy, bored). Even in those times when the suffering is not directly experienced, its potentiality is inherent in that matrix.

*   *   *

This causal vision also brings the Buddhist conception closer to the western scientific world outlook. All of science (with the curious exception of parts of quantum theory) has as its foundation "this is like this because that was like that." For example, the gravitational pull of the moon causes the tides, a spirochete causes syphilis, and optic-nerve firing causes activity in occipital cortex. In the 20th century, psychological processes have also come within this deterministic framework. Thus, two of the world's most influential psychological theorists, Sigmund Freud, the psychoanalyst, and B. F. Skinner, the Behaviorist, both characterize human activity as a product of specifiable dynamics. Both are self-described "determinists."

About 30 years ago, I was friendly with two people, a brother and sister, who were in their late 20s. They told me with bitterness about "Pop," their late father (he had been dead some 5 years), and about how much they hated him. He had tyrannized them. He had verbally and physically abused them. They described incidents of his throwing rocks at them and chasing them with knives. The son swore (the father, remember, was dead more than 5 years) "If Pop walked into this room, now I'd kill him." I later described this conversation to a colleague of mine, a clinical psychologist. He remarked, "I wonder what Pop's parents were like."

He was suggesting, of course, that Pop had not freely chosen to be a villainous child abuser. He had been molded by a set of conditions, including the way he himself had been raised, that stunted him. It left him with an uncontrollable temper and taught him only to use force with children.

Psychotherapists see patients with emotional problems. One of the standard concerns is what caused these problems. In short, modern psychology, like Buddhism, views the human as "caught" in a matrix of forces. These forces affect both the pain we experience and our actions.

FOR REFLECTION AND DISCUSSION

1. "The person in the world of Dukkha is like a leaf blown by the wind." This statement is, of course, a figure of speech. What is the intended meaning? Do you feel that this interpretation applies to your actions? Does it apply to you inner life (thoughts and emotions)? Explain your answers.

2. In the film scene cited, the warlord says "Many people hate me." Yet the Buddhist woman does not hate him. What is the difference between this Buddhist woman and the others?

3. You are right now reading this book. List all the things that *had* to happen in order for you to be doing this at this instant. Do you think you will ever finish this list?

8

The Noble Truth of Tanha (Craving)

The Truth of Tanha: We are vulnerable to suffering because of the way human nature is constituted. Specifically, we are a bundle of urges that push and pull from within.

The Buddha places the ultimate cause of suffering squarely within the individual. It is our cravings that keep us in Dukkha. This is an important shift of emphasis from the external to the more immediate internal cause of suffering. For example, we tend to think that being deprived of food is a cause of suffering. In the Buddhist view, it is the hunger we experience and the craving for food that is the immediate cause of our suffering. Deprivation of food is clearly a critical part of the causal sequence, but is one step removed from the final cause of suffering. I have known people who would periodically go on 3-day fasts, believing that this was healthy for the body. A common report was how wonderful (one of them used the term *euphoric*) they felt halfway through the fast. Clearly, deprivation of food for a couple of days is not, by itself, sufficient to cause suffering. On a fast, deprivation is clearly present. However, the craving for food, the final link in the chain leading to suffering, appears to be absent.

Again, we may think that a person who cheats us is the cause of our suffering. In the Buddhist view, it is our anger at being cheated, our craving to retrieve our money, our brooding over the event that is the immediate cause of our suffering. The fact of being cheated is an important event in the causal sequence, but is one step removed from the final cause of suffering. This view, then, focuses not on the external, more distant causes of our suffering, but on the immediate inner links of the causal chain, on our motivational and emotional makeup.

This contrast of outer and inner causes of suffering may be seen in the following Hindu tale:

An ancient forest hermit, with the begging bowl and the dress of a holy man, settled himself beneath a tree in the outskirts of a small city. He told the people who first saw him and who came to pay their respects that he would spend the season in this grove. Because this was considered a great blessing for the city, word was sent to the prince. On hearing the news, the prince felt that it would be proper for him to go out personally to welcome the saintly visitor. He gathered his guards and courtiers about him to take part in the procession. The prince and his retinue, arriving at the place to which they had been directed, found no one. They looked about fruitlessly until someone pointed up at the top of a tall tree. There, perched on one of the highest branches, was the visitor. The prince called up to him and introduced himself. After exchanging pleasantries of welcome the prince urged "Please come down. You are surely in danger sitting there like that." The old man responded, "I am not in half the danger that you are in oh Prince." "I?" exclaimed the startled prince. "These are my guards, the strongest in the land. My land extends further than the eye can see. What danger am I in?" The sage replied, "I speak of the dangers of anger, lust, and greed."

This tale brings out the subtlety of the Eastern view. For the prince, the outer world was well controlled. He saw, therefore, no risks, no danger to his well being. The sage, however, saw the dependence of happiness on the inner conditions—on the pushes and pulls of our being.

Just what are these cravings, these urges and passions that cause us pain? These amount to nothing less than almost the entire motivational system of the human being. It is worth, however, mentioning a few categories.

1. Basic biological needs. We are a species that has evolved and survived via sexual reproduction. Part of the mechanism for this is, of course, the sexual urge. Furthermore, we must live long enough to be able to reproduce. Therefore, we have evolved mechanisms for taking in energy (food and drink) to sustain ourselves, for organizing socially (family, group), and for escaping threats (pain, predators).

Within each of us, these mechanisms are manifested as urges: to obtain food, drink, sexuality, companionship, and children; to escape pain and to eliminate danger to our physical well-being. Whenever these urges are strong and unsatisfied, suffering is the likely experience.

Our biologically-based urges also include a variety of more or less conditioned reactions. When others frustrate us we experience anger; threats may evoke fear (or anger); mutilated forms or certain odors may produce feelings of disgust or aversion. Modern research suggests that the pain of boredom is also biologically based, that we are evolved to seek stimulation, to explore. Thus, our nature is such that biological forces can produce within us a variety of states that can range from unpleasant to acutely painful.

2. Ego needs. We strive for success and we fear failure. Like the little boy in class who waves his arm imploring "Teacher, call on me," we strive to show off. We seek praise and are pained by criticism. We're vulnerable to insults and put-downs; we become depressed or feel guilty when we've performed badly. In general, we strive to maintain and enhance a sense of self-worth, a striving that makes us vulnerable to mental pain.

3. Culture-conditioned needs. These take two forms. On the one hand, the culture we're born into has a system of values. Gradually, as we mature in this culture, it insinuates these values into our heads. We see these most obviously around sexuality. The 1930s middle-class

American culture, in which I grew up had me believe that promiscuous girls were bad, homosexuals were bad, and it was important that I marry a virgin. Such values not only make us vulnerable to pain but lead us to action—action that frequently causes pain in others.

Other examples are many and varied. Our culture—through its use of the media—stuffs into our heads the importance of striving for fashionable clothing, expensive cars, swimming pools, and so forth. Hollywood movies constantly used to show our glamorous film stars smoking, arousing the desire to imitate them.

A second form of the needs conditioned by our culture is, perhaps, more subtle. The Buddhists have pointed out that our concepts, the very terms in which we think, create needs and urges toward action. For example, our conceptual system fosters stereotypes of people different from ourselves, leading us to commit injustices against others, to experience anger and hatred against others, and to be victimized by others.

It is clear that there is a great variety of human motives. In fact, there is a Buddhist vow that begins "The number of passions is infinite. . . . " (This and other Buddhist vows are discussed in more detail later.) The passions we have reviewed are all potential sources of pain not only to ourselves but frequently to others whom we are impelled to hurt.

Of course, not all motives have this character. There are two other categories of motives that, it is fair to say, are not sources of Dukkha. These are what I call the gentle passions and the noble passions.

The gentle passions include desires to read, listen to music, and play a game. The character of these is that (a) we are not generally overwhelmed by a desperate urge to satisfy these needs, and (b) frustration of these needs is not especially painful. We want to listen to a Beethoven symphony and are about to play it on our stereo when we are interrupted. We generally do not find such a frustration particularly painful. In a way these gentle passions are ideal: We don't lust for the activity; we enjoy the satisfaction when it occurs; we are not pained when it does not occur. In the next chapter, where we discuss transforming the cravings, we do not necessarily mean having them disappear. Rather, we want them (cf. hunger, sexuality) to become like the gentle passions: We don't burn with need; we enjoy it when the need is being satisfied; we are comfortable when it is not. To put this another way, the eastern ideal is that our motives are no longer our masters, but our servants.

The second category of positive needs consists of the noble passions. These are of two types. First, there is the desire to become enlightened and liberated. No limits are placed on how strong this can be. Where other motives are to be reduced, this motive is to be encouraged. A senior monk told some novices:

"Imagine if your hair were on fire, how energetic and focused you would be to put that fire out. That is how you must strive for enlightenment."

The second type of noble passion is concerned with the world outside of ourselves, which I call altruism. It includes love, compassion, the desire to help others, and to correct injustice. We see this passion manifested at the very outset of Buddhism. Siddhartha has attained the deepest enlightenment. He recognizes that he is now freed of Dukkha. He is no longer vulnerable to the sufferings, large and small, that life can inflict. He can now, if he wishes, wander through life for the rest of his days, enjoying the "peace that passeth all understanding." He, however, does not do this. He recognizes that suffering is more abstract than his own personal experience. Yes, he is freed of suffering, but there are countless numbers of beings who are still in Dukkha. He decides, therefore, to return to the world and to teach. This became the model for later monks to follow. Other examples of altruism are shown throughout the book. Simply stated, one value in diminishing the cravings is that the altruistic passions can be more readily expressed.

FOR REFLECTION AND DISCUSSION

1. Monitor your own ego-needs. In the course of one week, count the number of times you say things just to show that you're not ignorant, that you're "in the know," or to just plain show off.

2. Human motivation was described with just a few categories (biological needs, ego needs, etc.) yet the Buddhist vow begins "The number of passions is infinite." In what sense are these two facts consistent?

9

The Noble Truth of Nirvana (Liberation), Part 1: Conquer the Beasts Within

The truth of Nirvana: We can attain freedom from Dukkha. We do this by changing ourselves, by transforming our cravings.

Buddhism does not contain only the dark view that we live in Dukkha, in the valley of tears. It also shows a way out. Because Dukkha derives from the maelstrom of cravings, urges, passions, and feelings, the way out requires putting an end to this turbulence. We must strive to reduce, minimize, even eliminate these inner pushes and pulls that seem to come from all directions. We need, in short, to transform ourselves. This emphasis may be seen in the following story:

In ancient India, a common sport had been for men to fight barehanded against tigers. One sturdy fellow, the world champion of his day, could vanquish even the largest, most vicious tigers, with little hurt to himself. One day a Hindu sage remarked to him "It is a great challenge you have met, to be able to master tigers. However, it is a greater challenge to be able to master yourself. Conquer the beasts within. That is the more difficult task." The champion's eyes were opened by this utterance. He took the sage as his teacher and started on the task of self-transformation.

A complete statement of the Buddhist vow mentioned in the preceding chapter is: "The number of passions is infinite; I vow to master them all."

In talking about "mastering the passions" it is essential that the proper interpretation be given. We in the West tend to think of "self-control." We will "control" our feelings of anger, "suppress" feelings of hunger or of fear. The Buddhist goal is not to *control* these urges but to *transform them*. The ideal is to have no feelings of anger, or hunger, or fear. In the West self-control implies that energy is exerted to keep the passions down. In the East, the passions are so calmed, so diminished in strength, that no energy is needed.

To illustrate this contrast let us consider an anger-provoking incident. Some fellow insults you. The Western view suggests that through gritted teeth and with clenched fists you keep saying to yourself "I won't become angry." In the Buddhist view of transformation, you simply do not experience anger. You deal with the situation appropriately, with intelligence, good humor, and even concern for the fellow. Anger isn't there. And, if someone should later compliment you on your handling the situation without anger or ill-will, you'd be surprised. The situation never struck you as one calling for anger.

Does this transformation seem difficult or even impossible to you? It does not come about simply by adopting the ideal of self-transformation. A commitment to change oneself is only the first step onto the path. After that, progress along the path requires years of effort and practice. It's very much like starting on a new skill such as playing the piano or skiing. Masters in these fields have so transformed themselves that, with seeming ease, they perform near miracles: playing a Beethoven sonata or gliding hundreds of feet through the air off a ski jump. You want to be such a master; that desire is the necessary first step. After that, much work—playing scales, practicing on the slopes—is required. Similarly, after commitment is made to transform oneself, to master the passions, much work is required. As we see with people who have put years of work into developing any skill, miraculous results can appear. In this case, the resulting miracle will be nothing less than liberation from Dukkha.

It is necessary to emphasize how radical a change in stance is this commitment to transform ourselves. Normally, we seek the cause of our unhappiness in external events.

"If only those blankety-blank neighbors would move away. Then I'd be happy."

"Damn right, I'm unhappy. My date stood me up."

"Sure I'm depressed. The editors rejected my manuscript."

"Of course I'm furious. He insulted me!"

According to the Eastern ideal, we need to seek the cause of our un-happiness within ourselves, in that inner, final link referred to in the last chapter. This is our job. If, in an intimidating or frustrating situa-tion, we become upset, we take this as a signal that further work on ourselves is needed. If we do not become upset, we may take this as a sign that our work is bearing fruit.

I once heard a Buddhist monk say that too much of what was writ-ten in Buddhism was for the training of the monks. His own Bud-dhist sect was concerned with the ordinary, lay people. "After all," he said "ordinary people have to deal with disappointments and anger." I perked up. Anger was then a kind of hobby of mine. I was interested in techniques for dealing with anger. I went up to him and asked, "What do you instruct people about anger?" He responded "We tell them 'When someone makes you angry your attitude should be: Thank you; you're my teacher.'"

This captures the essence of the Buddhist stance. When we in the West get angry, we see our task as getting even. We want to tell the other guy off, take revenge, or hurt him. The Buddhist stance is: Change your-self. That is your first responsibility. That is your lifelong task.

*   *   *

Western psychological systems also place great stress on a central motivational concept like urges or *drives* (the term most popular in these systems). In the behaviorist formulation there is a shift of em-phasis, however, which in turn, connects up with another Buddhist concept.

The Behaviorists sought to develop a language of observables such as "stimulus" and "response." They tried to avoid terms for inner processes, processes that couldn't be readily detected. The concept of *drive* posed a problem. The concept was obviously important but referred to something internal. Unless a person told us, or otherwise behaved in certain characteristic ways, we could not tell if the person was feeling hungry, or angry, and so forth. The solution for the behaviorist was to focus on goals. To every drive there is a corresponding goal or state of affairs, which can be more or less specified. Eating is the goal for hunger, mating is the goal for sexuality, and so forth. The Behaviorists used the term *reinforcers* to refer to these goals.

Just as the concept of craving is central for the Buddhist's understanding of the human circumstance, the concept of reinforcement has the same centrality for the Behaviorist. The Behaviorist thesis is that behavior is "shaped" by the reinforcers; it is organized around the attainment of the reinforcing states of affairs.

This tight connection between drive and the corresponding goal, permits a kind of translation of the Third Noble Truth. Instead of saying "Don't be so strongly pushed by your urges," one might equivalently say "Don't be so strongly pulled by the goals." The Buddhists, in fact, say this. A commonly heard Buddhist prescription is "Don't be attached." Don't be attached to any goal, to any state of affairs in the world. Transform yourself so that you can face with equanimity any change of circumstance, any loss, any failure to attain the goal.

Consider these examples: The swimmer who is in a funk because he didn't come in first in the race. The funk is produced by the attachment to winning, by the fact that winning has become so all-important to the swimmer. Coming in second, by itself, is not a sufficient cause of the funk.

A wife is unhappy because her husband wears old-fashioned suits. The unhappiness is produced by her attachment to fashion and to the good opinion of friends. Old-fashioned suits, by themselves, don't cause unhappiness. Nor (as children learn to tell themselves) do the words of opinion break bones.

Thus, the prescription to reduce the strength of the passions may be stated as the prescription to weaken the attachment to the goal (or reinforcing) states.

FOR REFLECTION AND DISCUSSION

1. "The beasts within." What meaning does this phrase have for you personally? What, in other words, are your "beasts"? Do you have techniques available for "conquering" those beasts? What are they? How effective are they?

2. "When someone makes you angry your attitude should be: Thank you; you're my teacher." What precondition is assumed by this statement? In other words, in what sense are you (the person who takes this attitude) a student?

3. Explain in your own words how the phrases "diminish the cravings" and "reduce attachments" are related.

10

The Noble Truth of
Nirvana, Part 2:
The Nature of Attachment

In the preceding chapter it was suggested that reducing cravings and reducing attachments are similar. Let us here consider further the latter sense of transforming oneself.

What are the full implications of reducing attachments? How does such a change relate to ordinary living, to the joys and goals of daily life? If I want to listen to a symphony, does that mean I am attached? If I look forward to enjoying a good meal, does that mean I am attached? That one can enjoy an event without being attached to it is suggested by the following observation from Buddhist literature.

The Buddhist monks normally obtain their food from farming, purchasing, or alms seeking. For this last method, the monk will go from house to house with a bowl, accepting whatever the householder will provide—a handful of rice, half of a potato, anything. Against this background are descriptions of persons of wealth who wish to honor the Buddha. Frequently, one or another will invite him and his followers to a feast on a prearranged day. The Buddha always accepts! How does this fact square with not being attached? Consider the following tale:

The Buddha and a dozen of his disciples take up temporary residence in the outskirts of a small city. The king, on hearing this, comes out to visit the Buddha. The king says, "It is a great blessing to us that you and your disciples are visiting. I would like to invite all of you to a dinner. I will have the palace chefs prepare a feast more splendid than has ever been seen in this kingdom." The Buddha accepts. The king suggests that on the following Tuesday, the Buddha and his followers are to come to the palace where the feast will be held.

This much is typical of the literature. Consider now this hypothetical scenario.

The appointed day arrives. The Buddha and his monks arise early and walk the distance to the palace, enjoying the pleasant morning. On arriving, however, they find that the palace gates are locked and that a large sign has been posted. The sign reads:

> Feast Canceled! Sorry, Oh Buddha,
> but the king was called out of town
> on emergency business.

Now, we can observe the absence of attachment. With no feelings of disappointment or regret, the Buddha turns to his disciples and says "Well, it's almost lunchtime. Let us go to the village houses and seek alms." We see him and the disciples leave as cheerfully as when they arrived, still enjoying the morning.

Giving up attachments does not mean giving up enjoyments of life's pleasures. It means, rather, never becoming *dependent* on the pleasures. It means being ready to forgo the pleasures without frustration. If a splendid meal is available, enjoy it; if not, be content with a humble meal. You've gotten tickets to this special concert? Wonderful! If not, find some other useful way to spend the evening. If you have nice clothes, enjoy them; if you have shabby clothes, ignore them.

What about long-range goals? If I want to be a doctor, many years of hard work are required. Doesn't such devotion require attachment?

"Devotion" and "attachment," however, are not synonymous. For example, I am a flutist. I have studied for many years. I am working out my own style of jazz-flute playing and am aiming at performance level. My goal, which I am still working at, is to play professionally. I practice hard. But I am keenly aware how fragile is this daydream, how vulnerable it is to loss. For example, if I break a finger the daydream is over. That awareness of fragility, that contemplation of the pitfalls along that path, helps to immunize me against the pain of loss. Along with the goal of becoming a flutist, is the larger goal of relating properly to that career. One must learn how to let go should it become necessary, how to walk away with equanimity, even with good cheer. Thus, one can be immersed in life, but can give up attachments.

FOR REFLECTION AND DISCUSSION

1. Someone says "I'm a hedonist. I live for life's pleasures." What two cautions would a Buddhist make toward such an attitude?
2. Distinguish between devotion and attachment. Do you currently have any long-range goals toward which you are working? Would you say you are "attached?" How can you tell?

11

The Buddha:
The Compassionate One

We have thus far reviewed the first three of the Noble Truths. These contain a certain conception, describing (1) Dukkha—the difficult situation the human is in, (2) Tanha—the passions as the essential cause of that situation, and (3) Nirvana—a way out, the possibility of transforming the passions. The fourth Noble Truth, which we have yet to review in detail, is not so much a part of the conception as it a set of methods for accomplishing the transformation. We will postpone consideration of these methods in order to discuss additional features of the general conception.

Two epithets are applied to the Buddha. One, as we have already seen, is The Enlightened One. The other, equally appropriate, is The Compassionate One. The Buddha's mission was to lift the burdens of suffering from the shoulders of everyone. When Siddhartha attained the ultimate enlightenment and became the Buddha, he did not conclude that his task was over. He had escaped from suffering but there were billions of creatures then and into the future who would still be in Dukkha. It was not enough for him to be satisfied with his own emancipation. Therefore, he turned to help others.

Compassion, for the Buddha, is not an arbitrary virtue. That is, he did not go about preaching "you should be compassionate," as though it were some independent principle added to his other teachings. Rather, compassion is an emotional, if not logical, consequence of having "in the bones" the knowledge inherent in the three Noble Truths. The Buddha has said that one sign that you are becoming enlightened, that is, that you are realizing the truth of that teaching, is that you are suffused with a sense of universal compassion. If, for each person you meet—whether stupid, hurtful, weak, or clumsy—you truly see how he is caught in the forces of Dukkha, feelings of compassion will be present. A vivid example of compassion-as-consequence was seen in the film scene described in chapter 7. A Buddhist devotee was challenged by the warlord who had earlier destroyed her family. Why, he wanted to know, didn't she show any hatred toward him. She, grasping completely the overwhelming forces (she called it "Karma") whose pawn he was, responded: "How can I hate you? You only did what your Karma made you do."

A second example of compassion may be seen in the following Buddhist tale:

In the woods near a village, were five soldiers, scouts from a neighboring army. Their orders were to obtain information about the activity in the village. Under no circumstance were they to permit themselves to be discovered; surprise was essential to the planned military operation. Their maneuver was almost completed when, to their chagrin, they were discovered. An old monk, while on a stroll from the village monastery, came upon them in the woods. The soldiers immediately captured him but recognized the awkwardness of their situation. They could not bring him back as a prisoner for that would reveal that they had clumsily let themselves be discovered. Nor could they leave him as a witness. That left only one alternative. Killing a monk, however, was a shameful action that not one of them would take on himself. They decided that all of them would share in the execution. They all confronted him, simultaneously drew their swords, and fell on him. They departed leaving him for dead.

Although dying, however, he was not dead. A short while later a few young monks passing by saw him on the ground and ran over to him. Kneeling around him they found him close to death. As he was dying, he whispered the events that had befallen him, and concluded his story and his life with the sentence: "Even as they pierced me with their swords, I felt only good will toward them."

A third example is found in the teachings and actions of Mahatma Gandhi. As we have pointed out, the Buddha was not the first person to claim that we live in the world of Dukkha. That view was part of the Hindu context in which he found himself. Within that context, a radical imperative was arrived at: We must not add needlessly to suffering in the world. If harm can be avoided, we must not harm others. This practice of being harmless was called *ahimsa*. It is a Hindu ideal even down to the present day. Gandhi insisted to his followers that ahimsa was fundamental to his political movement: One may break unjust laws, one may refuse to cooperate with unjust governments, but one may not be violent in the struggle. His entire political life was an example of ahimsa in action.

We have already referred to one of the vows, taken by advanced monks: "The number of passions is infinite; I vow to master them all." A second vow is taken in imitation of the Buddha and reflects the compassion inherent in the system. "The number of feeling, thinking beings is infinite; I vow to help them all."

The concept of compassion, then, is rich. It entails (a) feeling good will toward others, (b) practicing ahimsa, not adding needlessly to the suffering in the world, and (c) helping others. This compassionate sense arises when the Noble Truths are deeply understood.

*   *   *

Whenever I relate to an audience the tale of the old monk, I detect a gasp at the final line: "Even as they pierced me with their swords, I felt only good will toward them." It is one thing to practice detachment, but even to life itself? It is one thing to feel compassion, but even for one who is stabbing you?

I point out that we have a similar ideal, based on a similar view of human nature, in our own culture today. It appears in the relationship that psychotherapists have with their clients. I illustrate this with the following hypothetical, although realistic, therapy experience.

A psychologist is working in a prison doing therapy with some of the individual inmates. This, by itself, is a difficult circumstance. The psychologist insists that he needs to be alone with each client, that this is the only way to gain their trust. The warden insists that it is too dangerous for the therapist to be alone, unprotected, in a room with some of these inmates. They solve this dilemma by placing a button on the therapist's desk. When pushed, it sounds an alarm. Whenever the psychologist is doing therapy with an inmate, two guards will wait outside his office. Should the alarm sound, they are to come rushing in.

The therapist's client one day was a convicted murderer, known to have a violent temper. Therapy with this man had gone well for several sessions. At this particular session, however, the therapist asked what he thought was an innocent question but the prisoner became furious. He leapt across the desk, grabbed the psychologist by the throat, and started choking him. The therapist barely managed to reach the button. As soon as he pressed it, the guards dashed in, threw the prisoner to the floor, while the psychologist sank into his chair and recovered his breath.

Now . . . any psychologist worthy of the title will have as his first concern the well-being of his client. His response to the guards will be something like "Don't hurt him. Something went wrong. I don't know what it is yet, but somehow I must have touched a nerve."

The experienced psychologist, like the old monk, understands that the attacker's emotions and actions are the product of forces that brought him to this pitch. Such understanding dominates the psychologist's perception even when his own life is threatened.

Of course, it is rare that a client bodily attacks a therapist. What is common, however, is that a client attacks the therapist's ego. Clients frequently come in brimming with hostility generated over a lifetime, hostility they may not always be aware of. Frequently, this hostility erupts and is directed toward the therapist. The client may say angrily, "How could you ask me such a dumb question?" Or, "I've been to three therapists now. You're the worst of the lot." Therapists who take such attacks personally, and react defensively, or indignantly ("You've got some nerve talking to me like that!") need more training. They need to learn to see more deeply into human nature, to feel with greater empathy the forces that mold and push their clients.

Carl Rogers, an important theorist about the nature of psychotherapy, captured this spirit of concern for the client in a phrase that has become a therapy slogan. Our proper attitude toward our client, he said, is one of "unconditional positive regard" (Rogers, 1961). That "unconditional" echoes the Buddha's "universal" in speaking of compassion.

Both psychotherapists and Buddhists agree on the importance of seeing deeply into the matrix of forces that direct the inner life. Both conclude that when we achieve this, our compassion (good will, positive regard, concern) follows of necessity in an almost logical sense. They differ, however, in one way. Psychologists tend to think professionally, in terms of their clients. It is to these that they radiate positive regard. The Buddhist monk who is enlightened directs these sentiments toward everyone. Anyone who has contact with him is his "client." He vows "to help them all."

FOR REFLECTION AND DISCUSSION

1. The story of the old monk is a story of detachment. To what?
2. A parallel was drawn between the old monk and the psychotherapist. What differences would you say there are? Could you, personally, be a psychotherapist, responding with good will and concern toward angry clients? If yes, could you meet those challenges if they occurred now, in your everyday life?

12

Supermaturity

In the last chapter we suggested a parallel between Eastern and Western ideals. Both the Buddhist monk and the clinical psychologist work toward understanding the forces that determine the inner life. As a result, they both work toward behaving compassionately with others. The present chapter describes another ideal that we share with the Eastern tradition.

In our culture, it is good for an adult human to act like "a mature human being" and it is bad to act in an immature way. "You're being immature" is not simply a description but is a pejorative epithet—a criticism. Everyone I've ever suggested this to has agreed. For adults, being mature is good; being immature is bad. Here we seem to have a universal value.

When I present this assertion to one of my classes, say to my graduate students, they all nod in easy agreement. This is folk-psychology—familiar ground. But then I ask "What do we mean by maturity? Give me an example where you would particularly say of someone 'He's mature,' and then give me a general definition." Now a long silence follows. This is clearly not an easy question. You, the reader, might consider it now. See how you have to grapple to formulate an answer.

We can arrive at an answer by considering first the opposite. What do we mean by immaturity? When do we say that someone is behaving in an immature way? That's easier. A person is immature when he or she behaves, as we say, like a child (meaning, of course, the more unpleasant aspects of childish behavior). What are the hallmarks of this childish behavior? Here are a few: (a) Children want things now! Their cravings are such that they can't wait; (b) Children have temper tantrums over the most minor frustrations. Anger can run their behavior to a sometimes baffling degree; (c) Children do not spontaneously share and will frequently be seen pulling a toy or cookie out of another child's hands. Greed so dominates their behavior that they ignore the unhappiness of others; (d) Children frequently tease and make fun of and even bully other children. Ego needs push them to look better than other children to the point of being insensitive to the pain of these others; (e) Children are bad losers—and bad winners, for that matter. They grouse and grumble when they lose and gloat ("Ha, Ha. I beat you!") when they win. Again, their ego needs strongly run their behavior.

These are only some types of childish behavior. Of course, not all children show all these patterns and certainly not all the time, but they happen often enough that we readily associate them with children. Part of growing up is learning to (a) be patient without complaining, (b) control one's temper, (c) be fair with others, (d) be sensitive to the feelings of others, and (e) be good sports. In short, part of growing up entails learning some self-transformation.

When an adult has failed to learn one or more of these lessons, that person will, from time to time, behave "childishly." Thus, we are starting to get a sense of the meaning of immature behavior. The man who (a) fusses because his dinner is half-an-hour late, insisting he is "starving," or (b) is furious because someone cheated him out of a quarter, or (c) covets the goods of others and is stingy with his own, or (d) puts others down, laughs at others, tries always to be one-up, or (e) is a poor sport, cheats, and takes losing badly is said to be immature.

It is now easier to articulate when we say a person is acting "maturely." First of all, he has learned all the lessons of self-change that lead away from childish behavior. Of course, this is true of most adults. When, however, we say that being mature is an ideal, we mean something beyond normal adult behavior. When we say of someone that "he's being very mature about this," we intend that as a compliment. We mean that he is behaving well to a provocation or loss that would upset even normal adults.

We can now characterize three ways that adults might respond to a provoking event: childishly, normally, and maturely. These levels can be placed along a kind of scale as shown in the following examples.

A man with an income of $50,000 is cheated out of some money by another person, Mr. X. Mr. X. has left the country—he is gone forever. No strategy or even hope exists for getting the money back. Suppose the amount were $20.00. The childish person fusses noisily about being cheated; he obsesses, "If I ever get my hands in that guy. . . . " He generally makes the time unpleasant for people around him. Furthermore, he loses half a night's sleep berating himself for having been so trusting. He keeps imagining scenes in which he humiliates Mr. X.

By contrast, the normal adult would put it out of his mind. It's only $20.00. He readily sees how pathetic it is that someone would stoop to cheat for $20.00. Anyway, there is nothing to be done; it's history. He turns his attention to the present.

Suppose, instead, that the amount were $200. Now, if the person reacted with complaining and with loss of sleep, we would be more understanding. That, we would say, is a normal reaction. We would have been impressed, however, if he had shrugged it off, didn't let it ruin his (and our) evening, and had indicated that he sensed the desperation in Mr. X's action. This, we'd say, was a mature response. Thus, the more mature individuals can accept greater losses without being upset.

As we suggested at the outset, this ideal of becoming mature is similar to the Buddhist ideal of transforming oneself. The Eastern ideal, however, carries us further along the scale. Suppose the loss were $2,000. Now, we'd be understanding if even the most mature person were upset, if he fussed, and lost a night's sleep. But why, asks the Buddhist, should we draw a line between $200 and $2,000 dollars? Why not show equanimity—emotional poise, balance—to any amount of loss?[1] There is a Hindu saying: "If a man cheats you and

---

[1]We are here talking about a situation where it is clear that nothing can be done. It's a different matter if there are strategies (e.g., dealing with the person or going to the police) that might solve the problem. Such strategy-appropriate situations will be considered in Section 3.

you lose a night's sleep over it, then he's cheated you twice." Why be cheated of your inner peace by any amount of loss? The Eastern ideal means that we take our Western ideal of maturity and move it further along the scale, to what we here call *supermaturity*.

This scaled comparison between maturity and supermaturity applies to all the aspects of childishness. The mature person can tolerate necessary delays, and wait patiently, despite privations; the supermature person can tolerate even longer delays despite even greater privations. A Buddhist monk once wrote a poem whose refrain was "in waiting is freedom."

The mature person doesn't complain if his meal is late by hours; the supermature person doesn't complain if he must go without food for days. The mature person takes modest losses with equanimity. The supermature person takes all losses, big and small, with equanimity. The mature person puts the pleasure and pain of others as equally important to his own; the supermature person lives by the maxim: "Take joy in the joy of others; feel sorrow at the sorrow of others; care less about your own joy and sorrow."[2]

In general, a mature person feels disturbed (angry, impatient, envious) by fewer provoking events than a normal person; the supermature person has moved further along the scale and is disturbed by even fewer provoking events. As we transform ourselves, we move further along that scale.

We can view this scale, this comparison of the Eastern and Western ideal, in another way. The mature person experiences less inner turmoil and works more harmoniously with others than the immature person. It is fair to say, therefore, that the mature person is generally happier than the immature. Let us think, then, of our scale as a scale of happiness. This scale is shown in Fig. 12.1, which summarizes the relationships under discussion. At the extreme left is the happiness scale, going from some arbitrary low point up to some maximum (MAX). The left-hand panel shows the happiness over time of Person A, a normal adult. Happiness varies—now higher, now lower, depending upon events—around some intermediate level.

---

[2]This aphorism is cited as one of the Buddha's "great ethical principles" in a biography of King Mongkut, a 19th century Buddhist king of Siam (Moffat, 1961, p.17).

The next panel shows Person B, someone whose overall level has dropped. There is a great deal of anguish and turmoil in Person B's life. This is the typical person seen by a therapist or counselor. The therapist views his or her task as bringing Person B's overall level up to Person A's "normal" level.

The next panel shows Person C, who has greater maturity than the normal person (A). Person C shows less inner turmoil and he experiences more harmony with others. We are justified, therefore, in showing that his overall level of happiness is higher than that of the normal person.

We also suggested that Person C represents a widely held Western ideal. It is good to be mature, to be so transformed that minor frustrations can be tolerated with good cheer. The Buddhist asks: Why does our ideal reach only some level below the maximum? Why not aim at

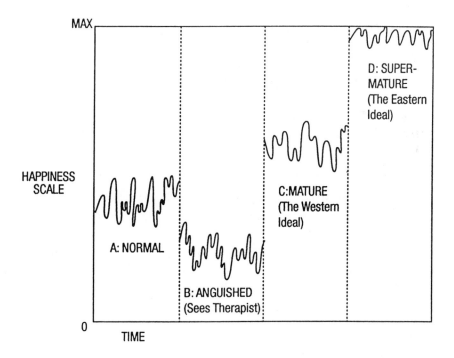

FIG. 12.1 The degree of happiness as it varies under four conditions.

the very maximum available to us as humans? On this view, even the people who reach the Western ideal (Panel C) are still subject to too many of the pushes and pulls of Dukkha. One can continue striving to bring the level even higher, to the realm of maximum harmony and minimum turmoil—panel D portrays this ideal. We characterize this state as supermaturity.

*   *   *

A difference here between the Western and the Eastern emphasis is worth noting. Traditionally, clinical psychology patterned itself after the medical profession. It was oriented toward helping people who were severely distressed psychologically and returning them to ordinary conditions of living—from Condition B to A in Fig. 12.1. The Eastern approach, on the other hand, is to help people go from ordinary conditions to enhanced conditions of living—from A (or B) to C and beyond.

In recent years an approach parallel to the latter has appeared in Western psychology. The movement began (arguably) with Abraham Maslow's work (1970) and, under the rubric of positive psychology, is currently fostered by Seligman (1999). Some aspects of this new approach are described in Part III.

FOR REFLECTION AND DISCUSSION

1. Five types of childish behavior were listed. Can you add other types to this list? For each of these types give a specific example. Then give an opposite example, that is, describe an action you would call "mature."
2. In waiting is freedom. Explain this expression. From what are you freed?
3. The mature person is generally happier than the immature. Do you agree with this? What arguments can you make in favor of the statement?

13

Anatman Reconsidered: You Are Not Your Mind

Buddhism, as we have seen, arose in a Hindu context and shares many of its ideals. At the outset, however, the Buddha announced one point of difference, the doctrine of Anatman. For the Hindu Yogi, the inner Atman constitutes the essential self. All other psychological processes, that is, our emotions and states of mind, are peripheral. The following example from Yoga practice will illustrate this idea.

Suppose you are starting the physical exercises of Yoga with a simple movement like raising your arms. You are instructed to breathe in slowly, raise your arms while inhaling, and lower them while exhaling. This cycle is repeated a few times. Simultaneous with this coordinated breathing and movement, you are to attend to and relax all muscles not in use (e.g., the face, the toes). Clearly, then, your mind is busy. It is focused on the movement, the breathing, the coordination, and the relaxing. Your full attention is required. Nevertheless, you may find your mind drifting, perhaps to a recent argument with your brother, or to the film you saw last night. In such a case, the beginner is instructed to redirect the mind. Specifically, you are to (inwardly) say "Stop," as though giving a command to a voice-operated TV set, and return to the movement, breathing, and relaxing.

Consider the psychological implications of this instruction. You are in two parts. There is your mind, which is either properly focused on breathing, moving, and relaxing, or is distracted by intrusive thoughts. Then there is that part of you that is monitoring your mind, observing whether it is properly focused or not. When necessary, it commands the mind to stop. It is this monitoring function that points to the more essential self. *You* are not your mind. The essential y*ou* is more anterior, capable of observing the mind's activities and, it would appear, of changing those activities. This anterior process, as we suggested in earlier chapters, is also capable of calming the mind and of assessing the beliefs held by the mind. It is that anterior process that constitutes the essential self and that ultimately points, in yogic belief, to the Atman.

The concept of Atman is like the concept of the eternal soul in that it is ultimately independent of the body, surviving the death of the body. The essential self, on the other hand, may also be thought of as a psychological process, as a "higher" part of the mind. This anterior or meta-mind may be considered a psychological function that observes and even controls the "lower" cognitive functions. Thus, one may postulate this anterior, more central psychological function without going beyond a naturalistic cosmology.

When the Buddha rejected the Atman concept, he created two problems for his philosophical system. First, the doctrine of Anatman appears to run counter to the doctrine of reincarnation. The king, Melinda, challenged the Buddhist monk, Nagasena, "If there is no Atman, what is reincarnated? What leaves one body and goes on to the next?" In my opinion, it is this difficulty that makes the concept of reincarnation less central, more dispensable, in Buddhism. The second problem concerns the essential self. It was not clear whether the concept of Anatman meant a denial also of the reality of the anterior psychological process that we have called the essential self. Critics occasionally write that "Buddhism teaches egolessness," an interpretation of Anatman as denial of the essential self in its psychological aspect.

However, as the yoga example suggested, that psychological aspect is too compelling to be ignored. As a result, later Buddhism developed a new concept, that of *Buddha-nature*. Buddha-nature is said to be inherent in all humans, waiting to be realized. It may be interpreted as that anterior, ideal, essential self: The more it is realized, the more we move along the path toward supermaturity. As we gradually calm the mind by transforming our passions, and gradually deepen our understanding, this Buddha-nature, this essential self, is said to be more and more revealed. The psychological aspect of Atman, therefore, returns in later Buddhism. Indeed, it was necessary to bring it back in, to do justice to our experience of inner duality: the observer and the mind that it observes.

*   *   *

The Behaviorist movement in contemporary psychology faced a challenge similar to that posed by the concept of Anatman in early Buddhism. One would think that any self-concept, because it has reference to an inner, not directly observable condition, would be dismissed by the Behaviorists. But B. F. Skinner (1965), one of the most rigorous Behaviorists, felt compelled to address this topic, notably in his *Science and Human Behavior.* Skinner was thorough in his determinist conception of animal (including human) behavior. He insisted that by knowing and by properly applying the laws of behavior we can raise happier human beings and can organize peaceful, well-run societies. The general thesis was that the psychologist (that is, the benign knower of the laws) would apply these laws to appropriately shape the behavior of others. But Skinner went a step further. He proposed that the concept of self-control is meaningful for the Behaviorist. It simply means that we take the laws as we know them and apply them not only to the behavior of others but to our own behavior as well. In a seminar that I attended with him, he gave this example:

Suppose I will be going to a party tonight and I don't want to get drunk. How can I control my drinking behavior at the party? Well, one rule that we know is that the thirstier you are, the higher the probability that you will drink. Conversely, the more your thirst is quenched, the lower the probability. Therefore, if I load myself up with liquid—drink a lot of water—just before going to the party, I will be less likely to drink anything at the party. Thus, I use behavioral principles to exercise self-control. Thus, I control my behavior.

Just as the Buddha spoke of self-transformation within a system of Anatman, Skinner spoke of self-control within a totally deterministic system. However, a problem similar to the Buddhist problem exists for the Behaviorist view. The statement "I control my behavior" has two self-references, "I" and "my behavior." But these have two different meanings. "I" refers to the controller, the one who knows the laws of behavior, sees how they relate to different problem situations, and applies those laws. "My behavior" refers to that which is controlled. The statement is parallel to the yogi who says, "I control my mind." "I" and "my mind," as we have seen, refer to two different psychological functions. Skinner, then, leaves us with the implication, awkward for a thoroughgoing determinist, that there is a function within us that can see, and even manipulate, the forces causing our behavior. That function understands and applies the laws instead of being moved by the laws. Surely, this implication is a challenge that needs to be confronted by the Behaviorist, or, indeed, by any deterministic point of view.

Let us illustrate this duality with another example, TV advertising. When constructing their commercials, advertisers use psychological principles such as fear-arousal appeals, or bandwagon claims, in order to influence viewers. If the viewer is ignorant of the principles, then he is vulnerable to the direct influence. If, however, the viewer, like the omniscient Behaviorist, is enlightened about the principles and can see their application in the commercial, then he is free of those influences. He is in a different place from the unenlightened. This comparison of duality is similar to the duality of self-control. The essential self, that part that knows the laws, is in a different place from the parts of the self that are being controlled. That essential self can influence the rest of the psyche and can thereby change the behavior.

The conception of inner duality appears also in modern Western psychotherapy. In a therapy relationship, therapists are always on guard against what Freud first characterized as counter-transference. During therapy, the therapist will strive to be in empathic communion with the client. Nevertheless, the therapist's own needs—to show off, to defend the ego, to seduce, to express anger, whatever—may intrude themselves as mental activity, with adverse consequences to the therapeutic process. Part of the training and the deepening enlightenment of the therapist concerns knowledge of the many subtle forms in which these needs can arise and intrude in therapy. The therapist becomes, hopefully, so transformed that during the therapy hour these needs do not arise. Of course, they always may, and so the therapist is always alert to their potential effect. He must recognize these effects when they occur, and quell them immediately, much like the yogi who says "Stop" to intrusive thoughts. And as with the yogi, we see the two parts of the psyche in operation, the need-produced thoughts themselves and the more anterior self. This is the part that, as enlightenment develops, monitors the mind and minimizes those unwanted thoughts.

The concept, then, of the essential self is alive and working in psychological thought both East and West. That self may be hidden, obscured by the activities of mind and emotion. But as we come to "know the laws," as we deepen our understanding of human nature and the human condition, and as we diminish the strength of needs and emotions, then wisdom and enlightenment become manifested. Synonymously, then the essential self is realized.

FOR REFLECTION AND DISCUSSION

1. "This mind is a theater." Explain this metaphor. Is there an audience? Is there a director?

2. Who are you? Write a letter to (an imaginary) new pen-pal in, say, Thailand. Tell that person who you are in as complete a description as you can. Where is the essential self in this description?

3. The chapter suggests that in studying psychology and in learning the laws of behavior, you can become free. Free from what? Give an example (different from those in the book) where it would make a difference.

14

The Noble Truth of Magga (The Path), Part 1: Wisdom and Ethics

The Truth of Magga: Liberation from Dukkha is attained by the practice of eight disciplines.

We are now completing our presentation of the Four Noble Truths. The first three Noble Truths (Dukkha, Tanha, Nirvana) were discussed in chapters 6 through 10. These together formed a general conception, a conception that was discussed in chapters 11 through 13. We now turn our attention to the fourth Noble Truth, concerning the eight-fold path that leads out of Dukkha. It is called eight-fold because there are eight disciplines that contribute to making progress on this path.[1] Following the suggestion by Rahula (1974), I group these eight into three categories: Wisdom and Ethics, which are discussed in this chapter, and Mental Discipline, reserved for chapter 15.

---

[1]"The path" is a common metaphor for personal development, although the "eight-fold" aspect is awkward. Another metaphor is "growth" into serenity, much like the emergence of a beautiful flower. With this metaphor, the variety of impor tant contributions (nutrients, water, sunlight, good seed) is more obvious.

Wisdom

1. Right Views. We must strive to see the truth of the world, that is, of the human circumstance, of ourselves, of those we come into contact with. The Buddha distinguishes two types of right views. First, we must see the necessity for behaving well with each other, for truthfulness, honesty, and harmlessness (ahimsa), for avoiding harmful gossip, ill will, seduction, and covetousness. The Buddha refers to these as the "worldly" right views and stresses their importance. These, of course, are all ethical imperatives, prescriptions for behaving well. Including them here under Right Views means that it is important not only to behave well but to understand the necessity for behaving well.

Still more important than these, however, are what he calls the exalted (or profound) right views. These are the views inherent in the Noble Truths. Progress on the path is made by absorbing these conceptions of the human condition and of human nature as deeply as possible, into our very bones.

2. Rights Thoughts. In the preceding chapter we discussed the inner duality, the distinction between the mind and the anterior self. As this self becomes more realized, the mind is seen more as its theater. The anterior self is not only the mind's audience but can be its director. The idea that "I" (the anterior self) should take responsibility for the thoughts active in my mind is consistent with this conception of inner duality.

Analogous to the distinction made for Right Views there are "worldly" and "exalted" right thoughts. Worldly right thoughts begin with eliminating wrong thoughts. Be on guard against all thoughts of ill will. Obsessing that "he insulted me," "he hurt me," "he cheated me" is, as the Buddha said, painful and profitless. Be on guard against thoughts of self-pity; don't wallow in guilt or worry or your own inadequacies. (Brooding, I like to say, is a Buddhist sin.) Be on guard, also against lustful and envious thoughts. These are all worldly wrong thoughts.

Worldly right thoughts, on the other hand, are planful. Suppose someone does something you find offensive. You don't want to be thinking angry, fearful, brooding, or obsessive thoughts, but you want to replace these with what I later call (chap. 28) a problem-solving stance. For example, suppose you are a relatively neat person but your roommate is a slob. You're unhappy about having to live among his scattered clothing and dirty dishes. In this situation, wrong thoughts would be angry thoughts and intimidated thoughts (fearful of his anger should you say anything). Planful thoughts concern how best to solve this problem. In this planning stage, you might think about the best way to approach the topic with your roommate. You can rehearse in anticipation the various turns the conversation may take. Think of possible compromises. Think about how to counter, with equanimity, his possible scorn or anger. You might also consider how to change yourself, such that you're less concerned with neatness. What perspective can you take such that you're less bothered by this environment? This problem-solving stance, this assessment of alternatives and rehearsal, constitutes worldly right thoughts.

Exalted right thoughts are connected to Right Views, to seeing people—others as well as ourselves—as caught in Dukkha. This will lead to more compassionate thoughts about the individuals. Also, thoughts of compassionate action in concrete instances can follow from thoughts about examples: the monk saying "Even as they pierced me with their swords I felt only good-will toward them"; the provoked person thinking "Thank you; you're my teacher"; the therapist showing positive regard even during the most hurtful insults; people who, in individual acts, have shown courage or wisdom or serenity. Meditating on these and similar models will help us think productively when challenging and troublesome events arise.

Ethics

3. Right Speech. We may distinguish two aspects of Right Speech. First, we strive to be trustworthy, speaking the truth even if it means personal loss. Second, we avoid speaking in ways that hurt others, such as malicious gossip, jokes at another's expense, catering to stereotypes or to racial bias. In general, avoid saying anything that would pit people against each other. To put this positively, cultivate a gentle, respectful style of speaking. Use speech to solve problems, to resolve differences, and to reduce hostility between people. A Western approach to right speech is presented in chapter 29.

4. Right Action. This is expressed in the word "ahimsa," (harmlessness, see chap. 11). Do not kill, hurt wantonly, steal, or seduce. This is worldly right action. Exalted right action reflects both compassion and liberation. Act to reduce the suffering of others, to reduce hostilities among peoples. Act courageously and with wisdom, untroubled by ego-needs, foolish fears, and personal cravings.

5. Right Livelihood. We are to gain our livelihoods without cheating or bribery, and with due concern for the rights and livelihood of others. In contemporary terms this includes not exploiting workers in your employ or the environment. Furthermore, we are to avoid occupations that are hurtful to others. Rahula includes here making or dealing in weapons, alcohol, and poisons. In its more exalted form, Right Livelihoods are those which serve others, occupations such as teaching, counseling, farming, building, and healing. It is acknowledged that one must support oneself and one's family, and that frequently one does not have a choice of occupation. But when there is a choice one should move toward right livelihoods.

Another aspect of Right Livelihood concerns one's attitude toward the work itself. Attention should be focused on the quality of the work and not on the goal—not on the salary or the reward. The work, no matter how humble, is to be treated with respect and commitment. This aspect of Right Livelihood is explained in greater detail in chapter 19.

FOR REFLECTION AND DISCUSSION

1. Notice the overlap in the eight-fold path with the Judeo–Christian Ten Commandments. How is the Buddhist treatment different? These injunctions, by telling us what not to do, help specify Right Action. Why then are they also mentioned under Right Views?

2. What in this chapter suggests the inner duality mentioned in the previous chapter?
3. One goal in Buddhism is to transform the cravings. How does practicing Right Speech and Right Action relate to this goal? To what other goal in Buddhism do they relate?

15

The Noble Truth of Magga, Part 2: Mental Discipline

Mental Discipline

6. Right Effort. We should direct our energies toward self-transformation. Recall the instructions of the senior monk: "Imagine if your hair were on fire, how energetic and focused you would be to put that fire out. That is how you must strive for enlightenment." (chap. 8) The Buddha noted that we are hindered in this task of self-transformation by five obstacles: sloth or torpor, agitation, ill will, doubt or discouragement, and lusting for pleasures. We must make every effort to dispel these, to continue our way toward the goal. This aspect of effort is quantitative; the sense is that we should marshal our energy in the service of becoming enlightened.

There is also, however, a qualitative sense to right effort. We might call it rightly directed effort. When we follow this path a change takes place in the way we relate to problems. When someone makes us angry, or hurts us, or embarrasses us, our tendency is to point to them, saying "you this" and "you that." Rightly directed effort is toward our own reactions, toward ourselves. Our first responsibility is to learn equanimity and patience. We saw examples earlier of this attitude: The Buddhist monk who advised: When someone makes you angry think "Thank you; you're my teacher," (chap. 9) and the Dalai Lama, who said: "The enemy can be very important; the enemy teaches you patience" (chap. 2). These examples neatly exemplify rightly directed effort, which is toward one's own reactions.

Let me add a personal example.

My late wife lived with the aftereffects of a brain injury for almost 2 years before she died. At times, her actions during this period were dangerous, at other times disruptive. Once, when we were about to leave for a doctor's appointment, I discovered she was not in the house. I dashed outside where I spotted her about two blocks away walking with her cane in her slow halting gait. I called to her and she stopped, turned, and started the slow walk back. As I strode toward her, I realized I was agitated and, yes, angry. My frustration had temporarily blanketed my "right views." I stopped, then, and took a breath. "She has become," I thought "my teacher." By the time we came together, I was able to greet her not with irritation but with concern.

Right Effort, the Buddha has noted, pervades the other seven strands of the path. We must direct our efforts toward all of these practices.

7. Right Mindfulness. We must be introspective in the context of living. The anthropologists have coined a useful phrase, the participant-observer. Anthropologists occasionally live in an exotic community for months and years. They may participate in it fully, taking part in rituals, going on hunts, and so forth. But all the time that they are participating they are also observing, gathering their information. Thus are we when we practice mindfulness. At the same time that we are active in the world, alone or relating to others, we must always strive to be aware. Be mindful of your speech and the effect it is having on others, be mindful of your thoughts, especially when they veer from right into wrong thoughts, be mindful of your views. Be mindful of your body in its humblest activities—eating, or brushing teeth. Be mindful of your feelings and emotions, those conditions under which your inner world becomes turbulent and those under which it becomes calm.

Clearly, mindfulness is an essential process in attaining self-transformation and enlightenment. It is through mindfulness that we come to verify the teachings. It also contributes to other components of the path. We must be mindful of our views, thoughts, speech, and actions.

As with Right Thoughts, Right Mindfulness suggests the inner duality, the idea that part of me can observe my mental and emotional activities. This constitutes further evidence that the Buddhist view implies an essential self, anterior to those other activities.

8. Right Meditation. You may have noticed, in the previous seven strands of the path, that they can be practiced in the every day activities. None of them conjures up an image, widely associated with Buddhism, of the practitioner seated fixedly in a meditative posture. This practice is a by-product of this eighth of the eight-fold path. It is an Eastern tradition that the meditator sits cross-legged, in what is called the lotus posture. As Rahula (1974) emphasized, however, the specific position is not essential. You can meditate while sitting comfortably in a chair or even while walking or eating.

Meditation as it is practiced in the East has many functions, but they may be grouped into four categories: focusing, developing mindfulness, desensitizing oneself, and seeking understanding.

Focusing. Focusing is a practice of stilling the mind. You sit quietly and select a point in the room to focus on. In yogic practice, a lit candle or flower may be used. You gaze at the candle and attend fully to it. Study the candle, become immersed in its flickering. Turn away intrusive thoughts and any sources of bodily tension. A more advanced form of this meditation is to focus not on an external object but on an internal image. With eyes closed, imagine a well-known object, for example, a candle, and hold this image steadily in your mind. These exercises are sometimes referred to as "calming" exercises, with the emphasis on calming the mental activity.

Developing mindfulness. Mindfulness meditation is the practice of becoming self-aware. It is directed at all aspects of our inner experience. There are three types of mindfulness meditations:

1. Bodily mindfulness. In one of the most common forms, the meditator sits and simply observes the breath. Inhaling slowly, one observes the bodily changes, how the air coming in massages the forehead, how the rib-cage expands. Exhaling slowly, one continues to note the various bodily changes. The meditator gives full awareness to repeated cycles of breathing. This is a meditation commonly recommended for beginning meditators. In addition to this breathing meditation, bodily mindfulness can be practiced during physical activities such as walking, eating, or brushing teeth. One consciously attends to what is happening to the body as one performs the activity.

2. Feelings mindfulness. One attends without judgement to feelings as they arise and as they disappear. One tries to be aware of even the most subtle feelings or emotions. For example, with respect to anger, one tries to be aware of the slightest irritation or minor tension. You want to become adept at always knowing what you are feeling. This kind of practice may be done when one sits quietly alone or in social situations.

3. Thought mindfulness. One observes one's own thoughts without censoring or prejudice or attempts at control. You want to become adept at always knowing what you are thinking. This is obviously a necessary skill in order to carry out the recommendations under Right Thoughts. This, too, can be practiced when sitting alone or when with others.

Desensitizing oneself. I have taken the term *desensitization* from Western psychology. When people have specific fears, such as, phobias, the therapist arranges for the individual to be exposed little by little to the feared object. The technique reduces or even eliminates the fear. In this particular meditation, one is to contemplate commonly feared and disturbing situations. Thus, one contemplates death in various forms, simultaneously reminding oneself that this is one's own fate. The aim is to free the meditator from turmoil at the thought of death, including his own death and those of people around him. One meditates on situations that arouse disgust, anger, fear, or pain, always with the ultimate aim of become liberated from these upsets.

Seeking understanding. This last category is what we in the West have traditionally understood by the term "meditation": One meditates about something, on some topic. Thus, one can meditate on the meaning of Dukkha or of interdependence. The French have a term *approfondir*, which means to strive to understand deeply, in a profound way. Such striving is a form of this type of meditation. Again, one need not sit in any particular posture. One can meditate while in a comfortable chair or while walking. I find that reading in the appropriate literature (philosophy or psychology) or preparing a relevant lecture is an effective stimulus to such meditation.

In one sense, the Buddhists go beyond Western meditation, that is, beyond striving to understand something. The advanced meditator seeks not only to understand but to *realize*. A particularly important topic for advanced meditation is Anatman (Sunyata in northern Buddhist traditions). The meditator strives not simply to understand the concept in some intellectual way, but to grasp fully, to *live* that condition. In meditating on compassion, the meditator may try to understand exactly what is meant by the concept or why it should be universally applied. But going beyond that, the meditator strives to feel and to radiate compassion and good will to any and all people.

Meditation is a large topic that has only been touched on here. The meditative process is discussed in greater detail in the next section on Yoga.

*   *   *

These, then, are the eight categories of activities that comprise the Four Noble Truths. All of these guide us toward self-transformation, toward strength and equanimity in life's turbulence, and toward maturity and serenity. My own experience is that different individuals find some of these eight strands more important than others. Just which ones are the most important varies with the individual. I, for example, tend to rank Right Views and Right Mindfulness as the most important activities. Many Buddhists, especially Zen practitioners, place heaviest stress on Right Meditation. Nevertheless, all eight are clearly important.

FOR REFLECTION AND DISCUSSION

1. What is meant by *"rightly directed effort"*? Illustrate your answer with an example from your own life where you either rightly directed your efforts or might have done so.
2. How would mindfulness be important if you were trying to end a habit such as smoking or drinking? Why, incidentally, would a Buddhist consider it important to end such habits?
3. How would bodily mindfulness help you realize that you were becoming angry? Why would this be important?

Poetry Interlude No. 1

TRANSCENDING

Escher got it right.
Men step down and yet rise up,
the hand is drawn by the hand it draws,
and a woman is poised
on her very own shoulders.

Without you and me this universe is simple,
run with the regularity of a prison.
Galaxies spin along stipulated arcs,
stars collapse at the specified hour,
crows u-turn south and monkeys rut on schedule.

But we, whom the Cosmos shaped for a billion years
to fit this place, we know it failed.
For we can reshape,
reach an arm through the bars
and, Escher-like, pull ourselves out.

And while whales feeding on mackerel
are confined forever in the sea,
we climb the waves,
look down from clouds.

From *Look Down From Clouds* (Levine, 1997). (Note: Escher's pictures frequently portray paradoxes.)

PART II
YOGA

16

Yoga and Buddhism

I suggested in chapter 4 that the Buddha was influenced by the philosophical Hinduism that was prevalent in his day. Some of the key concepts in that philosophy were Atman, Dukkha, Karma, and
reincarnation. There was also the belief that one's task in life is to
"purify" oneself. In Buddhism, this task became the Third Noble
Truth, that we are to transform ourselves, to diminish our cravings.
This philosophical Hinduism gave rise to Yoga, a system of thought
centered around the same key concepts. Yoga also took as central the
task of transforming oneself. Buddhism and Yoga, thus, are like cous-
ins.

There is also an important difference between Buddhism and
Yoga. Yoga includes the concept of Atman, of universal spirit. This
spirit is said to pervade everything in the universe including each one
of us. Thus, Atman can be thought of simultaneously as universal
spirit and as the individual soul.

Because of the belief in Atman, Yoga has two goals. One aim of
self-transformation is, as with Buddhism, liberation from Dukkha.
The second aim concerns Atman. One engages in self-transformation
in order to realize the Atman within. The mind, remember, was likened to a lake. When a lake is turbulent and stirred up, it is opaque.

When it is calm it becomes transparent. Only when the urges, agitations, worries, and so forth are calmed can Atman be "seen." A Yoga practitioner may pursue either goal, striving to end suffering or to realize Atman. Clearly, these two pursuits are intertwined. Realizing Atman, like ending one's suffering, entails reducing cravings and clearing the mind of misconceptions. The same self-transformation that produces liberation from Dukkha permits realization of Atman.

Buddhism, it would appear, has only one goal, liberation from Dukkha. But Buddhist practice does have a second aim, one that parallels striving for Atman. Understanding this requires a deeper understanding of the concept of liberation (Nirvana). Suppose all our cravings are subdued, all our misconceptions are dispelled; we are liberated. What is our psychological state? We may think of Nirvana here as peace, as a deep inner serenity, as the "peace that passeth all understanding." In their meditative practices Buddhists can strive to realize that state directly. Thus, while Buddhism teaches liberation from Dukkha, it also proclaims that a remarkable serenity will result. The Buddhist practitioner may meditate to realize directly that serenity.

In addition to liberation from Dukkha, both Buddhism and Yoga have, then, a second aim. In Buddhism one strives to realize that special psychological state. In Yoga one realized Atman. Although similar, these two experiences are different in one obvious respect. Realization of Atman is frankly spiritual. Yoga is presented here primarily as a system for eliminating inner suffering. The religious aspect, however, adds interesting psychological features.

The term "Yoga" means "linking" and is linguistically related to the English term "yoking." One interpretation is that the inner and outer Atman are to be linked. The Yoga master, Desikachar (1977), presents another interpretation, that the anterior part of ourselves (the source of mindfulness, the part that monitors our thoughts) is to be better linked to our behavior. This "linking" is another way of expressing communion and liberation, the two yogic goals of self-transformation.

There are several types of Yoga practices to help reach these goals. Some of these are:

1. Hatha Yoga. The Yoga of purification. This is the Yoga most familiar in the west, the Yoga of postures, relaxation, and diet.

Hatha Yoga begins with the body and its care. As the next chapter illustrates, this is only the beginning.

2. Jnana Yoga. The Yoga of wisdom. This stresses studying the psychological and philosophical literature, striving for the attainment of Right Views. These right views include realizing Atman.

3. Bhakti Yoga. The Yoga of devotion. Atman is to be realized in direct attempts at communing with deity. Inner change is sought directly through prayer or religious ecstasy.

4. Karma Yoga. The Yoga of action. One immerses oneself in higher social purposes. Mahatma Gandhi, in his selfless, fearless pursuit of social justice, exemplified Karma Yoga.[1]

Of course, these modes are not mutually exclusive. As with the eight-fold path, one can pursue them simultaneously. Our discussion is centered around Hatha Yoga, since that is best known in the West. It will be clear, however, that these different approaches are sensibly contained within a single framework.

FOR REFLECTION AND DISCUSSION

1. In Yoga, when you reduce the cravings and clear the mind of conditioned beliefs and restless thoughts, you are in a new state, one in which you are better able to realize Atman. The Buddhist's do not use the concept of Atman. How would they describe that new state? Compare the two interpretations.

2. Four types of Yoga were described. How do they relate to the Buddhist eight-fold path?

---

[1]Note that "Mahatma" is not Gandhi's first name, but is a term of honor meaning Great (Maha) Soul (Atman). It emphasizes the spirituality manifested by this man of action.

17

I Discover Hatha Yoga

In my late 30s I began to be troubled by various aches and ailments. The most serious of these, heart palpitations, sent me running to my doctor. He checked me over and reassured me that the palpitations were not serious. They and the occasional pains in my shoulder, neck, and knee were common with people coming into middle years. I was aging, he suggested, and I had to accept that fact. This diagnosis and advice was repeated a year later by another doctor when I moved to another part of the country. I grimly resigned myself to aging.

Shortly after visiting the second doctor, I discovered an early morning television program on Yoga by Richard Hittleman. Although I had been reading Buddhist and Hindu literature for a few years, this was my first contact with Hatha Yoga. Hittleman demonstrated various simple postures (asanas) and described the procedures for entering, holding, and emerging from each asana. These procedures are generally the same for each pose, and may be illustrated with a simple movement, raising the arms above the head.

Begin with your arms relaxed at your sides and exhale as completely as possible. When you are at the bottom of your breath, begin to inhale slowly; simultaneously raise your arms until your hands are pointing up to the ceiling. The movement is slow,

85

and is coordinated with the breath inhalation so that you attain the desired pose at about the time that your lungs are full of air. Hold your breath and the posture for a few seconds, then exhale slowly, simultaneously lowering your arms, reaching the starting position at about the same time that the breath is completely exhaled. Repeat the cycle three or four times.

While performing this coordination of breath and movement, two other tasks are required. First, any muscles not in use are to be relaxed. For this particular exercise, for example, you are not using your face muscles or your toes. Attend, therefore, to your forehead; feel it relax. Wiggle your toes a bit; make sure they're loose. Second, you must be mindful of your mental activity. Attention is to be focused on the breath-movement coordination and on relaxing. The immersion in the body should be total. Should your mind start to wander, or you find yourself thinking about a political issue, for example, or a problem at work, you are to silently command "Stop" and to refocus on the bodily activity.

After watching for a couple of mornings, I decided to try the simple movement that I just described. It felt wonderful, astonishingly wonderful. The slow tempo, the relaxedness, the gentle massage of my pajamas slowly sliding along my body, all combined to produce instant satisfaction. I repeated this movement a few times, savoring the pleasure. After that, I started watching the program more closely, selecting other simple asanas to perform, gradually expanding my repertoire. Soon I was spending half-an-hour each morning, repeating 3 or 4 times some half-dozen postures.

There are enough (actually dozens of) asanas that on different days I could perform different sequences. Some involved neck muscles (turning the head), some the torso (turning the body, bending), and some the finer muscles (flexing fingers). There are standing postures, sitting postures, and some lying on the floor postures. I've heard the asana system described as slow calisthenics, but it goes beyond that. The system seeks out every muscle and exercises it. There are asanas that exercise the face muscles, the toes, even the tongue! An introductory set of asanas may be found in Hittleman (1969) and in Christensen (1987).

A number of effects and insights resulted from this daily half-hour of practice.

1. The most dramatic change concerned my health. After just 1 month, all my ailments—the aches and sudden pains, the heart palpitations — disappeared. It felt as if the movements had oiled my joints, so that I now moved smoothly and easily. The doctors had been wrong: I hadn't been aging; I had been rusting. It was as though every muscle from my heart to my limbs had been operating under too much internal friction. These systematic turns, bends, and stretches had lubricated the system.

The physical benefits after that first month went beyond the disappearance of the ailments. I moved more easily and with more of a spring to my step. I felt younger. After a month, I felt like I was 18. I remember thinking "I suppose after 2 months of practice I'll feel like I'm 12. And what after that?" I had discovered the fountain of youth.

About 6 months after I started practicing Yoga, my father, who was then 65, complained to me of a neck ailment. Whenever he sat in one position—reading a book, watching TV, driving a car—his neck "froze up" on him. It was excruciatingly painful when, after sitting still for a few minutes, he turned his head. His doctor's diagnosis was no more helpful to him than mine had been to me: He was old; he had to resign himself. When my dad told me of his trouble, I suspected that Yoga would help him. The notion of "Yoga," however, had for him the same forbidding exoticism as voodoo or black magic. I merely advised him "When you get out of bed in the morning, while your neck is still normal, spend 5 minutes exercising your neck in slow motion. Turn your head from side to side, lift your shoulders and role your head in the cradle that they form. Add any other neck-and-head movements that feel good."

Two weeks later he phoned, exulting that the ailment had vanished. He intoned "You're in possession of a great secret."

Such was the ignorance about exercise 30 years ago.[1]

---

[1]My and my father's experiences occurred in the late 1960s. Today the physical benefits of Yoga are commonly accepted by the medical profession. Yoga postures (Ornish, 1990) or Yoga-like postures (Egoscue and Gittines, 1998) are used for heart ailments and for chronic pain, respectively. Physical therapy, a profession little known 30 years ago, also utilizes similar movements.

2. The slow breaths were also important. An automobile offers a useful analogy. A badly tuned car will still run and take you places. If you tune the engine, however, it will run more smoothly, more economically, and will last longer. The slow breathing has a parallel effect. Our normal inner rhythms may not be quite right, although we function adequately. Slow breathing seems to correct those rhythms; it "tunes" the body (see Berger & Owen, 1992).

The next time you are agitated, and you feel that your inner rhythms are out of kilter, try slow breathing. Exhale all your breath and then breathe in slowly. Feel how the air, as it goes through your nostrils, gently massages the inner forehead; feel the air slowly fill your body. When you reach the top of the breath, hold it for a few seconds then breathe out slowly with the same attention. See whether, after three or four such breaths, the agitation hasn't changed. My own application of this technique is described in Part IV, where I discuss handling anger.

3. I found that I was sleeping better and, consequently, was needing less sleep. I had been practicing Yoga between 30 and 60 minutes each morning. The problem of where I was going to find the time in what was already a busy schedule took care of itself. My sleep habits changed; I needed less sleep. Other practitioners have told me of a similar experience, that sleep was sounder and more efficient. Being "too busy" is probably not an adequate reason for avoiding this exercise.

4. Serious Yoga practitioners can assume striking, extreme positions. Two examples are shown in Fig. 17.1. The beginner is cautioned, however, to treat these models as ideals and not as challenges to be immediately mastered. You can hurt yourself if you try the advanced asanas before you're ready. In Yoga, you must never strain yourself. You move in the direction of the ideal, but stop at that final comfortable point. If you're feeling pain or even strain, you have moved too far. As an example, consider a simple turning movement. Standing with feet planted firmly on the ground and with hands on hips, turn the torso slowly to the left with the head turning to look over the left shoulder. Advanced Yoga practitioners can turn and hold a pose well in excess of 90 degrees. Suppose you can turn comfortably only through about 60 degrees. Stop there. Over time your body will attain greater flexibility. For now, however, work within your current limitations.

FIG. 17.1 Two examples of advanced Yoga postures (Photos by DeSciose, from *Power Yoga* by B. B. Birch, 1995). Reprinted with permission.

It is the antithesis of Yoga to criticize yourself or berate yourself for "failing" (not fully reaching the demonstrated pose). A Yoga teacher used to tell each of the students in his group "You are perfect." Each one was to be working within the confines of his or her own body, and not to be comparing and pejoratively judging. In this connection, a subtle but important distinction is made. You assess but you do not judge. You have an image of the ideal posture (in the previous example, a 90-degree turn) and a sense of where you are (app. 60 degrees). You are to note and assess this difference and over weeks and months strive toward the ideal, but you are not to "judge" yourself in any harsh, critical manner. The latter are Wrong Thoughts that only amplify Dukkha.

5. Yoga is currently popular in America as a discipline leading to health and well-being. As important as this is, it is a secondary goal. Unlike calisthenics, which you may perform while watching television, in Yoga you focus on what you are doing. Furthermore, you are simultaneously slowing the body's rhythms, what I referred to earlier as tuning the body. This combination of being immersed in your action, while the inner tempo is calm I call the yogic state. In doing the postures, you are practicing a skill: getting into and staying in this state. The performance of asanas, then, not only betters your body but gradually improves your ability to be in the Yogic state. In this state, remember, you are calmly immersed, undistracted by hungers, thoughts, or resentments. This inner transformation, one of the central goals of Buddhism and Yoga, is taking place while we improve our bodies. I sometimes think that the remarkable changes that can occur in the body (see again Fig. 17.1) are meant to symbolize the even more remarkable transformation on the inside.

This increasing facility to be in the Yogic state has significance beyond the half-hour of asana practice—it transfers to daily living. Again, the outer symbolizes the inner. Just as we will move through the day more smoothly and easily, we will also focus on our daily activities more calmly and completely.

FOR REFLECTION AND DISCUSSION

1. You were annoyed with someone and said something more hurtful to them than you really intended. What would your feelings

be like? Regarding your reaction to what you said, distinguish between judgment and assessment.

2. Yoga is different from calisthenics in that the Yoga movements are done more slowly. In what other ways are they different?

3. Sitting alone comfortably in a chair, take four or five long, slow breaths. Follow the breaths; relax your muscles. Afterwards, write a paragraph describing the experience.

18

Savarasana

One of the Yoga postures, called Savarasana, is completely different from the others and has its own particular effects. I describe it as the dead-weight pose but that is not quite the literal translation.

This is not a movement but a state of being. Wearing loose clothing, lie flat on your back on a comfortable surface (e.g., a rug, a mattress, even a grassy lawn), arms at your sides, legs slightly apart. Your eyes may be open or closed (I prefer keeping them open). There should be an awareness that your head, body, arms, and legs are all in contact with and supported by that surface. Imagine that the surface you are lying on is gently rising up, like a mythical flying carpet, and that gravity is pulling you flat against it. You, in short, are to become a dead weight, without any muscle tension in your head or limbs.

While movement is not part of this asana, breathing certainly is. You take the usual long slow breaths, feeling the air massage your forehead, feeling your rib cage slowly expand and contract. And you simultaneously focus on relaxing. Recall, that for any asana, muscles not in use are to be relaxed. Since none of your muscles are required for this asana, you seek to relax all of them. Between the long, slow breaths and the total relaxation you are, in effect, putting your body into the condition of deep sleep.

Your mind, on the other hand, is to stay awake and focused. Ideally, it should be attentive to the activities of breathing and relaxing. One way to focus is to count your breaths. I do this in one of two ways:

I count "1001, 1002, 1003, . . . " at about one count per second for the first breath, "2001, 2002, . . . " for the second, "3001, 3002, . . . " for the third, and so on. In this way, I not only keep track of the number of breaths I have taken but I also measure how many seconds, loosely speaking, each inhale–exhale cycle lasts. (Each complete breath takes me about 30 seconds.) While I am counting I also feel the air massaging my (inner) head as I inhale and imagine it washing over my limbs as I exhale. This imagining greatly facilitates relaxing.

Or, I use visual imagery in the counting. I picture an object or event that rhymes with the number of the breath. Thus, for the first breath (one) I picture a bun, keeping the image of that sandwich-roll before me for the entire cycle of the breath. For breath two I picture a shoe, for three a tree, for four a door, and so on up to ten, when I picture a pen. Then I start over. Again, I also focus on relaxing while using this system.

Notice that I always know how long (roughly), I've been in this state. If I want to arise after 10 minutes I simply count 20 breaths.

This combination of putting one's body to sleep, so to speak, but keeping the mind awake, has remarkable effects. After 10 to 15 minutes I arise feeling refreshed, as though I had just had an hour's nap. In fact, it is better than a nap. There is no transition of sluggishness or inertia that often follows a nap. Right after doing Savarasana, I am clear-headed and alert. If I am tired during the day, doing Savarasana is like a nap, enhancing my energy and my mental clarity, but it requires much less time.

A second effect of doing Savarasana is in the experience itself. You sense the body going to sleep. Input from the body ceases. I no longer know if my hands are touching my thighs or if they are spread apart. Just how wide apart are my legs? I have no idea. Movement, however, can still be controlled. I end the posture after, say, 20 breaths, by first wiggling my toes and fingers. But movement breaks the spell so I use it only when I want to arise. Although input from my limbs ceases, the other senses continue to function. I keep my eyes open, and am able to see (usually the ceiling, or the sky). I can hear. I tell my wife that she can ask me a question. I can hear it and remember it. But I can't answer it until I "awaken." The movement of speaking would take me out of the state.

Savarasana shares with all the other asanas the aim that one be completely immersed in the process (here, counting or imaging, breathing, and relaxing). In this connection, the literal meaning of the term "Savarasana" is relevant. Earlier in this chapter, I called it the dead-weight pose. In fact, the term more literally translates as the death (or corpse) pose. When I first employed the literal translation, my listeners didn't want to hear me any further. The phrase evoked a negative emotional reaction. And so I started using "dead-weight," which people found more congenial. My listeners were no longer put off. But the literal meaning adds another component, one that facilitates immersion. Death, of course, is a condition that separates us from the cares of life. Suppose someone owes you money. Once you are dead that is no longer your problem. Similarly, in performing Savarasana the sense should be that your daily cares are no longer (for that 15-minute interval) your problem. For example, when I'm lying flat in that state, I might hear my children squabbling outside. It is no longer my problem. The thought intrudes that my neighbor insulted me. It is no longer my concern. For those 15 minutes I am in another place, separated from the cares of life. This attitude, that one is as dead, is obviously a valuable technique for focusing, for turning away from the distractions of the senses and the mind.

Learning to think of Savarasana as the death pose has another benefit. Naive listeners have a rejecting, emotional reaction to the phrase. We are all conditioned by our culture and possibly by our biology to find thoughts of death and dying upsetting. This fear-and-upset reaction is obviously a source of suffering that we, in our search for serenity, would do well to overcome. The attitude that in performing Savarasana, we are taking the death pose helps do just that. We become a little more emotionally *desensitized* (see chap. 15) to the concept of death. We can start to think about it more comfortably.

*   *   *

In recent years a Hindu guru, Maharishi Mahesh Yogi, began preaching in the United States about the benefits of Savarasana. He called it Transcendental Meditation (TM) and emphasized the energy and mental clarity that the practice produced. Also, the daily period of deep relaxation was said to benefit the body. In order to keep the mind awake during the deep relaxation, the practitioner was to keep repeating mentally a mantra (an aphorism, or inspirational sentence, usually in Sanskrit).

At this time, Dr. Herbert Benson, a researcher at Harvard Medical School, was working on the causes and cures of high blood pressure. A few TM practitioners presented themselves to him and suggested that this meditative practice lowered blood pressure. They, themselves, had low blood pressure and Benson looked into their claim. He found that by training people in TM, which he began calling the Relaxation Response, blood pressure could, indeed, be lowered. Benson saw that the specific mental act of reciting a mantra was not necessary. What was important, however, was to keep the mind active during the relaxation process. He then substituted counting breaths for the mantra. This has been his procedure ever since (Benson, 1975).

Over time, Benson (1987) has broadened the application of the Relaxation Response. He reviews research suggesting its benefits for a variety of physical and psychological ailments. Furthermore, he shows that young people who start practicing the Relaxation Response improve in their academic performance. This squares with my own experience of the mental clarity that follows practicing Savarasana. More recent research (Smith, Compton, & West, 1995) demonstrates that this type of meditation also enhances one's sense of well-being.

FOR REFLECTION AND DISCUSSION

1. This chapter implies that normal, nighttime sleep consists of two components. What are they? Are both necessary for the restoration of energy that sleep produces? Why, or why not?
2. What was your own reaction to learning that Savarasana means "death pose?" Would that affect your willingness to try the practice? Suppose you felt some reluctance; how would that relate to the Four Noble Truths?

19

The Yogic State, Part 1: Immersion

What are we practicing when we spend an hour doing different asanas? On the surface, we are practicing movements aimed at making our bodies more flexible. Also, we are practicing slow, deep breathing for its physiological benefits. This is on the surface. On the inside we are practicing certain skills. Most importantly, we are practicing focusing, immersing ourselves completely in the activity. Ideally, all of the mental activity is directed exclusively to moving, breathing, and relaxing. There is no fear, agitation, craving, or any other condition characterized as Dukkha. This chapter and chapter 21 deal with implications of this practice. We are also learning to be without pejorative judgment. The significance of this practice is discussed in the next chapter.

If one considers the asanas as an outsider, observing only what can be seen, they appear to be a dull, tedious activity: Raise the arms, lower the arms, turn to the right, turn to the left. There is nothing with any intrinsic intellectual fascination. Nevertheless, the Yoga exercises are not boring; one does not feel restless or impatient. The reason is that we are completely immersed in the process. The mind is so busy attending to the breathing, moving, and relaxing that there is no room for impatient thoughts. And if any negative thoughts do appear, we turn from them, bringing ourselves back to the immersed state. Now many, if not most, of our activities in life are equally dull and tedious. We go up stairs and down stairs, put on and take off clothes, pull up weeds, take out garbage, and so forth. What I started to find was that this Yogic state, this condition of calm attentiveness, was transferable to daily living. Here is a representative example.

> I needed to go up the stairs in my house to get something. At that time my wife, who had an injured leg, couldn't use the stairs. I told her that I was going upstairs and asked if there was anything she needed. She said that there was not and so I went up, retrieving what I was looking for. When I descended my wife said "Honey, there is something I need. Would you mind getting it?" Before even a twinge of irritation could arise I said to myself "Think of it as Yoga." While going up the steps, I focused on my breath, the movements, the relaxing in Yogic fashion, and was as much immersed and at peace as when I was doing any asana. There were no thoughts that this is "bad" or "wasteful," no resentment or grumbling. It was no more significant than if I had been asked to demonstrate a Yoga movement.

And another:

> I returned home after a long day that included teaching an evening course. It was about 10:30 p.m. and my wife was comfortably settled into the couch, watching a television show that I like. I wanted to be with my wife and watch the show. However, I did not want to fall asleep on the couch fully clothed, teeth unbrushed, generally unprepared for bed. So I decided to first brush my teeth and to change into pajamas. The next 10 minutes were revealing. When I started, in some haste, the brushing and changing, my mind was entirely on my wife and on the show that I was missing. My state was one of frustration: I didn't want to be here, doing this; I wanted to be in the living room.

> I didn't like this state of impatience and frustration. I found it unpleasant. And so I decided to treat these activities—brushing teeth, changing clothes—as Yogic activities. I began by taking

long, slow breaths. With awareness of these breaths, I attended to putting the toothpaste neatly on the brush. I focused on my teeth as they were being brushed, on carefully unbuttoning my shirt, on hanging up my clothes. Exactly as with the asanas, everything else disappeared. For that 10 minutes, there were no impatient thoughts of waiting wife and television show. There was no feeling of frustration, none at all. Instead, there was the calmness of the Yogic state.

More generally:

I need to clean a stack of pots and pans, a job of perhaps half an hour. I give myself over to it completely, attentive to every detail. There are no thoughts that "this is a bore" or "this is a waste of my valuable time." There is no unhappiness at all. There is no room for unhappy feelings, so engrossed do I become in the task.

It's easy for me to tell when I am *not* in the yogic state. I feel rushed. I move suddenly. I grab objects or slam them down with too much energy. I fumble, drop things, tear things. My mind is elsewhere, perhaps thinking about tomorrow's meeting for which I am now, with unnecessary haste, preparing those papers. Fumbling or over-energetic movement is a signal to slow down, to retune with proper breathing the inner rhythms, and to get into the task at hand.

All this I learned for myself. It was a personal discovery that my morning Yoga practice had transformative effects extending into my daily life. I later learned, with no great surprise, that this quality of immersion in one's activities was a Buddhist-yogic ideal. The Eastern literature contained several examples.

A young monk, camping near the edge of a precipice, realized that he had been discovered by a distant tiger. The beast was now bounding toward him. The canyon prevented any escape, but looking over the edge the monk saw a few inches of rock jutting out about 6 feet below. As luck had it, there was also a shrub growing out from the side of the cliff just below his feet. He used the shrub to climb down and then clung to it while he perched on the short span of rock. Above him appeared the tiger's head peering greedily; below him was a sheer drop to the distant boulders. The monk thought "I hope he tires before I do." Waiting, thus, between tiger and ravine, the monk noticed that this shrub was a strawberry bush and that some of the berries were large and ripe. With a free hand he plucked one and bit into it. He was amazed at how sweet and juicy it was. He savored fully its perfumed flavor.

Here is the same tale in a different form:

A monk, crossing a footbridge across a ravine, was enjoying the beautiful scenery. When he was halfway across, the footbridge broke. As he fell, he continued to enjoy the view.

And then there is a Japanese Haiku:

Placing the goldfish bowl carefully upon the ground, he turned and ran to help with the burning building.

I particularly like this last example. We can see the fellow, in all the bustle about him, taking the required moment to give the goldfish bowl its full due.

A Zen Buddhist once said, "Don't be split." He meant that you should avoid thinking about one thing while doing another. When you are brushing your teeth do just that rather than thinking impatiently about what is ahead. When setting down the goldfish bowl, give it all your attention.

The sense of immersion without inner distraction is particularly important in work and daily obligations. Thich Nhat Hanh, the Vietnamese Buddhist monk, advised: "Do the dishes as though you were washing the baby Buddha." Thomas Merton, the Catholic philosopher, made a similar suggestion: "Make a chair as though an angel were going to sit on it."

Attend to each detail lovingly, carefully, without thought of time or sacrifice. Let your task, whatever it is, be a labor of love.

In the great Hindu religious work, The Bhagavad Gita, the god Krishna teaches the disciple Arjuna to work for the sake of the work, and not for the sake of the goal. The goal may be important, but the means, the process of attaining the goal, has its own importance and deserves attention. Immerse yourself in the process itself.

Life, of course, is full of these means–ends relations, from opening a package of tea, to working for one's salary, to becoming a doctor. I sometimes speak of the attentive, "unsplit" practice as the Yoga of opening packages. The next time you open a package of tea, for example, change your approach. The common attitude is to get at what's inside, forgetting everything else. Instead, give the work of opening the package all your attention. While taking long, slow breaths, open the package carefully, neatly. Engage the task, as though it were a work of art. See how the impatience to get at the contents disappears. And, incidentally, as a by-product, you will have a better looking package, one that will be easier to close and reseal.

One particular means is waiting. We frequently have to wait—at the doctor's office, on line at the supermarket—to reach our goal. If you are required to wait (e.g., the line at the supermarket checkout counter is extra long) and you are thinking impatiently about where you have to get to or all the important things you have to do, then you are "split." You are now here on line. Find interesting ways to fill the time, in conversation, for example, or reading. If there is nothing at hand, you can always turn to deep breathing, to retune the rhythms of your body and mind. How patiently you wait is a good index of how much progress you have made toward self-transformation. A Buddhist monk wrote a poem with the repeated refrain: *In waiting is freedom.*

There are several advantages to being immersed in life's activities. First, as the previous examples indicate, you are at peace within yourself. The inner tempo is calm; there is no sense of conflict or danger, no feeling of frustration that you're not elsewhere. Closely allied to this inner calmness is your relation to others. You become much more patient with people. I gave the example of my wife having me make a second trip up the stairs. But people or circumstances again and again require us to do extra chores, or wait, or take a circuitous route. When we treat these tasks as yogic activities, we treat them without judgment. They are not intrinsically bad. Hence, we are less likely to be irritated or impatient.

Another advantage of immersing yourself in your activities is that you do better work. As I previously stated, there is less fumbling, tearing, and dropping.

My first sense of this came when I was in the army, before I knew anything about Yoga. Our platoon had a daily calisthenics session during which we were shoeless and shirtless, stripped to our pants. At the end of each session, the sergeant would announce "Last one dressed goes on K.P." As you might expect, everyone rushed to get his clothes on. At the first two experiences with this new challenge, I saw that the fellow who "lost" (first session) hadn't buttoned his shirt properly, and (second session) was fumbling badly with his shoe-laces. I realized then that I needn't hurry. I simply must not fumble or make mistakes. Each day after that at the appointed signal, I dressed very carefully with full attention to what I was doing. I was never even close to last. Invariably, one of the "rushers" went on K.P.

In all the examples of immersion thus far, the individual is alone in relation to inner process (performing asanas, meditating) or to objects in the world (putting on clothes, doing the dishes). However, another advantage to being immersed in activities is social. When we are with other people we want to immerse ourselves, to be fully "in" the relationship. During his or her training, the clinical psychologist learns to attend exclusively to the client, to see the client's world, to be empathic with the client's emotions. Of course, such a manner of focused relating, of being empathic and attentive to others, is available to all of us. When it happens, it is an uncannily rich, intimate experience.

So much so that Martin Buber, a philosopher writing in the early part of this century, singled out this way of relating, calling it the I–Thou experience (Buber, 1937). He exalted this connecting, this empathic communion, as one of life's ideals. The essence of it is immersion, the same immersion as that practiced in meditation or the asanas. As the skill generalizes to the world, it generalizes to the social world as well.

*   *   *

We are coming to learn today that immersion is a key to creative thought and problem solving. An early indication is in an 1879 newspaper description of Thomas Edison: Alone by himself . . .

sits the inventor, with pencil and paper, drawing, figuring, pondering. In these moments he is rarely disturbed. If any important question of construction arises on which his advice is necessary the workmen wait. Sometimes they wait for hours in idleness, but at the laboratory such idleness is considered far more profitable than any interference with the inventor while he is in the throes of invention. (Friedel, 1992)

A more recent testimonial was by Edwin Land, another distinguished inventor (Polaroid sunglasses, the Land camera). He said that when he was in a creative state, he would not permit himself to be interrupted by anything. No telephone was in his workshop; no person was permitted to intrude. He did not think even about eating. So fruitful is this condition of being "into" a task, he suggested, that one must resist being pulled out of it.

This suggestion has recently been investigated more formally by Csikszentmihalyi (1990). He interviewed many creative people in depth, including sculptors, composers, authors, and scientists. He inquired into personality traits as well as into working styles. Although these individuals differed radically from each other, they had one quality in common. They all immersed themselves in their work. They could be that way for hours, and felt that that is when they did their best work. Also, they all reported enjoying that state. Being in it was for them one of life's highs. Csikszentmihalyi wrote of this state (he called it "flow"): "one acts with a deep but effortless involvement that removes from awareness the worries and frustrations of everyday life," and "concern for the self disappears" (p 49). It would appear that there is no "split."

In my own book on problem solving (Levine, 1994) I proposed a principle of Intimate Engagement. The first essential step in solving a problem is to immerse yourself, to engage the problem intimately, with zest. This is described as giving the time and the energy needed to explore the problem–situation fully, from all angles. The effectiveness of this immersing approach was demonstrated with examples ranging from repairing a clothes dryer to solving a math problem. The psychiatrist Scott Peck in The Road Less Traveled (1978, p. 28) suggested a similar principle.

FOR REFLECTION AND DISCUSSION

1. What are the advantages of immersion? Think of immersion as a skill. What might you do to get better at it?
2. Describe an activity that you found agitating or frustrating. Replay that scene using the recommendations discussed in this chapter. How do the changes relate to the Four Noble Truths?

20

The Yogic State, Part 2: Transforming Judgment

I suggested earlier that the practice of asanas has two types of benefits, outer and inner. The outer benefits are better health, a sense of well-being, and, from Savarasana, mental alertness. These are short-term benefits in the sense that if Yoga practice is discontinued, these benefits will tend to disappear. The inner (and long-range) benefits derive from skills that are being practiced internally as we perform the asanas. One of these skills, immersing oneself totally in the task at hand, was discussed in the preceding chapter. The other skill consists in practicing a new attitude. In Yoga we learn not to be judgmental. Initially, this practice is focused on ourselves. Suppose I am unable to perform perfectly the demonstrated posture. If I am unhappy with myself, that is judgment. Also, if I am doing the posture perfectly and am wishing that everyone is watching me, that, too, is judgment. These complaints and cravings are not part of the yogic state. In performing Yoga, one is practicing eliminating these judgments.

Instead of judging, we assess. In performing a particular posture, we have the ideal in mind and move in the direction of that ideal. We hold the posture just a bit (1%, I like to say) beyond the limits of our comfort, and do not strain. If we are only halfway to the ideal that's fine. With continued practice, we will find that the limits of comfort move closer to the ideal. The ideal is there for us as a target, so to speak, toward which our match comes closer and closer. Thus, by assessment we mean noting the discrepancy between the attained and the ideal, and using that difference as a signal of what needs to be done. Pejorative judgments are irrelevant; they are only another source of Dukkha.

This attitude is appropriate to our progress on the path in general. Let us assume we are committed to the task of self-transformation. We have in mind an idealized version of what the goal is like, that is, of how an enlightened person would behave. When we, in our own behavior find that we are a good distance from that ideal, we do not come down harshly on ourselves. Rather, we take that shortcoming as a signal to study within ourselves what are the obstacles and how we may circumvent them. Consider this example. The enlightened person understands the matrix of forces in which people are caught. He or she, therefore, feels compassion and goodwill toward everyone. We, on the other hand, may find that we are reacting emotionally and with bias against a person's affectation, weight, color, voice quality, or mannerism. ("Look at the jerk! An American speaking with an artificial British accent. Who does he think he's fooling?") That inner revulsion that we experience is clearly a lapse from the ideal of seeing the person deeply. When we recognize it as a lapse, however, we are not to follow it by self-flagellation, discouragement, or harsh self-criticism. Adding such pejorative self-judgment to the revulsion only compounds the Dukkha. Rather, the experience of revulsion is a signal that we are still some distance from the goal. It is a signal on which to meditate, in order to determine the causes within ourselves of that negative reaction, to dig out the obstacle on the path.

The practice of being nonjudgmental during the asanas generalizes not only to our own personal shortcomings, but to the way we relate to the world. As we saw in the preceding chapter, life imposes on us many meaningless, tedious tasks. If you must spend an hour mowing the lawn, beware of judgmental thoughts: "This is a waste of my time; this is stupid; this is too boring." Such judgmental thoughts are, as the Buddha says, painful and profitless. With continued Yoga practice, pejorative thoughts while performing work, duties, or chores start to dwindle away. And, by immersing yourself in the task, you eliminate these thoughts along with boredom and resentment.

Eliminating pejorative judgment generalizes, perhaps most significantly, to the way we relate to other people. Yoga teachers, for example, approach their students uncritically. That is why they can teach "you are perfect." Assess, yes. They will guide the student to move toward the ideal. To scoff, sneer, discourage, or fail to suffer fools, however, is not part of Yoga teaching.

In its application to others, the new attitude—assessing instead of judging—works hand in hand with attaining right views. By giving up judgment in our stance toward others, we facilitate seeing them properly. We have a better sense of the matrix of forces in which they are acting. Judging others harshly, dismissively, and otherwise pejoratively, obscures our vision.

Substituting assessment and appropriate action for judging and for the risk of inappropriate action thus benefits the individual in two ways: There is less inner turmoil and one's relation with others improves.

*   *   *

This habit of replacing assessment for judgment, which we practice during the asanas, has its counterpart in Western teaching. Perhaps the oldest and most famous instance is Jesus' injunction, don't judge: "Judge not, that you be not judged" and "Remove the mote, etc. . . ." Another popular form is the Native American saying "Don't judge a man until you have walked a mile in his moccasins." The sense of this is that we should empathize as much as possible with the other, get a feel for the forces acting on him, before rushing to judgment. It is echoed in still another Western saying "To understand is to forgive" (although the Eastern version probably would be "To understand is to see that forgiveness is irrelevant." (see example on p. 28, "How can I hate you?")

This suggestion, that we not judge others, runs a risk of being misinterpreted. At this point, one of my students will generally ask "What about a man who deliberately hurts others or who generally does something bad. Shouldn't we have feelings of revulsion toward him? Shouldn't we be judging him?" Consistent with the outlook developed throughout this book, the answer to both questions is "no."

Feelings of revulsion and pejorative judgment of that individual is inappropriate. Answering thus, however, does not mean that we ignore hurtful actions or that we are advocating permissiveness and inaction. This entire book has from its beginnings, emphasized concern with suffering, and with reducing it. The ideal world would have the minimum of suffering. Anyone who goes against that ideal, who amplifies needless suffering, must be stopped. We take action not only to stop that person but, hopefully, to teach that person. Suppose, for example, that a child gratuitously hurts an animal. It is inappropriate to have nasty thoughts about the child. It is, however, appropriate to stop the child, and to teach that child that such actions are not to be repeated. To perceive the child as "bad," however, is not appropriate. Equally inappropriate is the cluster of negative emotional reactions that go with such a perception.

Assessing instead of judging is to be used not only with children. If a grown man hurts an animal, we might be more puzzled than if a child did it. With a child we can grasp that the mind (or brain, if you prefer) is as yet unshaped by the forces of socialization. Hence, biological forces inherent in his nervous system dominate his behavior. With the adult, however, we assume that efforts at socialization have been made and so it is harder to grasp the forces driving his behavior. They are, nonetheless, there. Hence, we assess the action, stop or prevent the action, and try to get the individual to change his ways (what I loosely call "teach"). If the man's actions are dangerous (produce a lot of needless suffering) he may even have to be isolated from the community. And as with the child, we act not vengefully, but with concern.

This attitude—taking action against a perpetrator without pejorative judgment of that individual—was summed up by Gandhi with an old aphorism: "Hate the sin and not the sinner." A modern language variation was presented by Zimbardo and Gerrig (1999), who described the contemporary professional attitude toward punishment: "Punishment should be a response to specific undesirable behaviors and never to a person's character." (p. 251)

FOR REFLECTION AND DISCUSSION

1. If you are like most of us you occasionally react with negative feelings toward someone because of his or her weight, facial

features, way of speaking, sexual orientation, or race. Describe in detail a couple of recent occasions when you reacted in this way. (You may not want to do this publicly but be honest about it with yourself.)

2. Consider the instances when you have reacted negatively. What would a Buddhist say about such a reaction? What would a yogi add about such a reaction? What can you do to decrease the likelihood of such implicit judging?

3. Think of someone (either from memory or from imagination) who occasionally does something terrible. Describe your emotional reaction to that person. How would you apply the aphorism "Hate the sin and not the sinner"? Suppose you saw the person frequently. According to that aphorism (and the Buddhist-yogic techniques, generally) how should you relate to him or her? (Keep in mind that this will depend on what, exactly, those terrible actions are.)

21

The Yogic State, Part 3:
Life Is Where You Find It

In the preceding chapters, I showed that practicing the Yoga postures entails practicing being in the yogic state. Furthermore, I suggested that this practice is transformative, that we can readily enter the yogic state for all kinds of daily activities. The activities I described—going upstairs, waiting on line, working on some project—tended to be brief and episodic. However, this psychological condition of focused attention, of feeling calm and relaxed, of being nonjudgmental, is relevant to the most fundamental conditions of living.

I discovered this for myself in an incident about 15 years ago. My daughter, then in her early 20s, woke me from a sound sleep at about 2 a.m. on a cold, snowy night. She had just gotten home, and was breathlessly frantic as she spoke to me. Her car had stalled in the snow in the middle of a hill not far from the house. She was not able to restart the engine or to budge the car. It now blocked the road. She ended with "Dad, you've got to help me." After putting on boots and my winter coat, I found a couple of snow shovels and went out with her into the storm. The car was indeed stuck in a drift in the middle of the road. We shoveled around the tires for some 10 minutes. Then, because the car was on a hill, I was able to push it back down while she maneuvered the steering wheel. Together we rolled the car off to the side of the road.

During this entire process, she was furious, cursing non-stop. Looking at her I realized something about my own inner state: I wasn't angry. Here, through no fault of my own, I had been roused out of a warm bed to go out into a storm to push a car. Yet I wasn't angry. In fact, I looked at my daughter as she fumed, and thought, "What is there to be angry about? We have to do this. Let's just finish the job and go back to the house."

Although I hadn't particularly tried to produce it, I saw that I had the right stance. Life had placed me in the middle of a snowstorm with a job to do. It wasn't good and it wasn't bad. Judgment was irrelevant. I simply had to face the problems of this new situation and do what was needed to be done.

Then, in the swirling snow of this dark night, I had an epiphany. This episode, I saw, was the paradigm for life's changes. A job cut-back, a car accident, a mugger with a gun, might, in a moment, change my life. It is pointless to curse my fate, to harp on its being "bad." I am simply in a new place with new challenges, and new problems that must be faced. This insight could be summed up with two words: *Stop judging.* Wherever life places you, that is where you are. Simply deal with that; deal with it in the yogic state.

I might well have applied this insight earlier in my life, when I was rudely pulled out of one circumstance and dumped into another. In my mid-20s, I was employed as a civilian researcher at an air force laboratory. Lieutenants and captains were my colleagues. People like corporals and sergeants served us by taking the tests we were fashioning. The Korean War was then in progress and in spite of my research so essential to national security, I was drafted into the army. Suddenly, I was a private, at the bottom of the ladder. The corporals and sergeants lorded it over me and verbally abused me. They did this, of course, to all the new soldiers in my basic training company. I was resentful, however, that I was being bossed by people who owed me, the great scientist, proper respect.

I was resentful, yes, and miserable, a condition, I now see, that was completely unnecessary. I was in a new place and simply had to deal with the challenges of that new place, with no looking back, no regrets, no complaints. At that time, alas, I lacked that insight, and suffered needlessly.

*   *   *

Suppose that through some freak hostage-taking situation, or some social upheaval, you are placed in solitary confinement. This is surely a situation in which most of your supports for conventional happiness have been taken away. People, nevertheless, have reported seeing even this as a situation with challenges (Csikszentmihalyi, 1990, pp. 90–93). The problem of boredom must be faced. Several ex-prisoners have described taking this problem-solving stance and arriving at various solutions. One proved geometry theorems to himself, another played chess games in her head, another imagined himself playing 18 holes of golf (!) every day. The novelist, Solzhenitsyn, described how, in a Soviet prison his mind was filled with poetic images and novelistic scenes. "The head count of prisoners remained unchanged but I was actually away on a distant flight" (Csikszentmihalyi, 1990, p. 92). Even planning and putting into execution ingenious ways of escaping is a problem-oriented approach. It is the emotional baggage of anger, gloom, and brooding that pulls us out of the yogic state.

FOR REFLECTION AND DISCUSSION

1. Think of times in your adult life when conditions changed for the worse—an accident, or a loss, or just plain bad luck. What was your emotional reaction to each event? What is the meaning of "don't judge" in relation to those events? Would it make sense for all of them? If not, why not? In general, are there times when it is actually desirable to experience the painful emotion?
2. What are the ingredients of the yogic state? Describe these as you would to someone who knows little about Yoga.

22

Yogic Theory:
The Unenlightened Mind

Much of this book thus far can be summarized in what I call the Yogic theory of mind. The theory first describes the mind before enlightenment. It specifies what needs to be done to transform the mind, and then describes the mind after enlightenment. The conception of mind before any enlightenment has taken place is the focus of this chapter. The mind and consequent behavior after enlightenment, after one has transformed oneself is discussed in the chapters that follow.[1]

Figure 22.1 portrays the ordinary mind before there is any awakening or enlightenment. At the left we see information entering either via the senses or from memory. This information impacts on a

---

[1]I rely heavily in this section on the Bhagavad Gita (Herman, 1973) and on the writings of Patanjali (Bahm, 1961), particularly as they have been interpreted by T.K.V. Desikachar (1976). Desikachar is an Indian master who has an excellent grasp of American culture. He presented his conception of Yoga during a series of lectures at Colgate University. While I draw on these and other authors, I inevitably contribute my own interpretation. For example, Figures 22.1 and 25.1 are my own devising. I can only hope, as I have throughout the entire book, that Eastern scholars will not find me too far off the mark.

Before

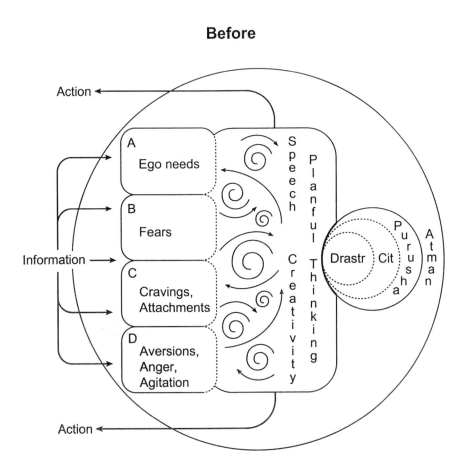

FIG. 22.1 The Yogic conception of the mind before it is enlightened. Information interacts with the passions (A through D), and beliefs and attitudes (spirals). These influence cognitive functioning. Anterior processes (Purusha) are nonfunctional.

two-part system. One part of the system is the passions, prominent here as it is in Buddhism. Somewhat analytically, here the passions are divided into four categories: ego needs, fears, attachments, and aversions, labeled A through D. They clearly influence how one interprets and emotionally reacts to the incoming information. For example, one might see an insect and react with disgust. Or, remembering a sarcastic remark by an acquaintance, one might become angry. The second part of the system is the mind proper, or more precisely, *the conditioned mind*. The unenlightened mind is entirely conditioned by its culture, language, and biology. As we have discussed in earlier chapters, these influences infiltrate into our minds as beliefs, values, prejudices, rules for "proper" behavior, habits of thought, tastes, likes, and dislikes. All these conditioned values, notions, and habits are shown in Fig. 22.1 as spirals representing whirlpools. That is, they are both structured and highly energetic. They strongly influence the thought processes. In addition to these are the restless, distracting activities of the mind, the compulsive brooding, the inner dialogues, the succession of memories. The Rosicrucians called it "grasshopper mind." The Yoga teacher Richard Hittleman spoke of the untransformed mind as a tape recorder that is constantly running. This property is represented by the long arrows.

As we move toward the right in the figure, we move toward processes that start to offer the possibilities of enlightenment, namely speech, creativity, and the ability to solve problems; what I call "planful thinking". In the unenlightened mind, however, these are either unused, or are impaired by the misinterpretations produced by the passions and the conditioned mind. Thus, one acts, as we say, without thinking. Or the person reacts immediately from impulse and desire, without considering the long-term consequences. Or he produces elaborate arguments to defend arbitrary if not foolish ideas.

Notice one last feature of the mind proper. It is the source of action. The nature of the action will, of course, be dictated by the passions and the conditioning-filtered interpretations. There is no guarantee that these actions will reduce Dukkha; they frequently will have the opposite effect.

This overview of the active part of the unlightenment mind—the passions, the conditioned beliefs, and the biased or bypassed thinking—is complete. This cluster of processes is self-contained. It generates action, for better or for worse. There is, however, an additional set of processes that are potential but in the unenlightened mind, fail to function. They are shown at the right in Fig. 22.1. The continual movements of the mind—information coming in, generating emotions, interacting with beliefs, producing thoughts and responses—block out these more anterior processes. Let us nevertheless, consider them here.

From time to time we have referred to the anterior functioning of the self. During an asana, for example, part of us monitors the activity of the mind, keeping it focused on the movement and the breathing, guarding against intrusive thoughts. In discussing Right Thoughts we suggested that part of us is observing the thoughts that occur, replacing inappropriate negative thoughts with appropriate positive thoughts. Also, we pointed out that the psychotherapist must be aware of his or her own emotional reactions and biases against the client. These must be shunted aside so that they don't interfere with the proper therapeutic response. In all of these examples, there is the idea both of the functioning mind and of a more anterior part of the self that monitors and, if necessary, alters the mind's activities.

Yogic theory deals explicitly with this idea of the anterior self, using several concepts. (Note: the terms are Sanskrit words.) First there is the witness or seer (Drastr; see Fig. 22.1). This is the part of us that is capable of observing the mind's activities. Cognitive psychologists have recently been employing the concept of the "mind's eye," a concept that would not be too different from Drastr. Along with witnessing, with observing the mind's activities, comes Cit, the ability to reflect or meditate upon that which is observed. For example, a psychotherapist might note within herself a twinge of resentment evoked by a client's remark. She might later ponder on why that feeling of resentment arose. The self-observation reflects Drastr. The subsequent self-exploration reflects the activity of Cit.

Both processes are part of Purusha, a complex concept that can be understood both psychologically and metaphysically. In the psychological sense, Purusha not only observes (Drastr) and contemplates (Cit) the mind but also guides it. It is that part of ourselves that grasps wisdom and liberation. Just as the Yoga teacher specifies an ideal posture that we, perhaps over months or years, strive to attain, so Purusha understands and can represent to us the ideal condition of enlightenment that we can strive to attain. Purusha, thus, is capable of altering the mind. It does this both by representing the ideal and by directly changing mental process, redirecting one's lagging attention, for example, during the practice of a Yoga posture.

In the psychological sense, then, Purusha observes, reflects upon, and alters the mind's processes. Remember, however, that Purusha doesn't function when the mind is completely unenlightened. As the metaphor of the lake (p. 81) suggested, the turbulence of such a mind prevents the Purusha processes from being experienced. It is when Purusha begins to be realized and to function that the individual begins to change. He can then start to assess how far his mind is from the ideal condition.

I stated that Purusha has not only the psychological functions just described but can also be understood as a metaphysical concept. In the metaphysical sense, Purusha is similar to the Western idea of soul. In this sense it hints of the divine, of a part of ourselves unconditioned by worldly events, a part that lasts beyond the death of the body. Notice that the psychological and metaphysical aspects of Purusha are separable. One need not believe in an essence that lasts beyond the body, but one can still believe in a psychological process that can observe, meditate upon, and ultimately reshape many of the mind's processes. In this latter sense, that is, psychological without the metaphysics, the concept of Purusha is congenial with the Western scientific outlook. Recent authors, for example, have started to write about metacognition and about executive functions of mind that oversee and affect lower level cognitive functions (Nelso, 1992). It is also congenial with the Buddhist concept of Buddha-nature, which we are all said to have and which is the ideal to be realized.

Finally, there is the concept of Atman in which everything is said to be embedded. Atman is purely metaphysical. If Purusha is soul then Atman may be thought of as spirit. It pervades all and, as such, is within us. The difference between the Atman within us and the metaphysical aspect of Purusha is not always clear. (How clear is the difference between the terms soul and spirit?) Some authors use them interchangeably. For Desikachar (1977), for example, everything anterior is Purusha; he never mentions Atman.

We may, I think, safely assume that the metaphysical aspect of Purusha is synonymous with the Atman within. When the Buddhists characterize their outlook as one of Anatman, it is this metaphysical sense that is given up. The concept of Buddha-nature may be seen as similar to Purusha in its psychological properties. Both psychologies, then, emphasize this anterior part of the self, this ultimate source of wisdom, this part to be realized.

The conception of Purusha enriches the view of human nature as it has thus far been characterized. Until now we have emphasized that the individual is "caught in a matrix of forces," is pushed and pulled by these forces. This view applies, of course, to the unenlightened individual. The further he or she is from the goal of self-transformation the more relevant is such a causal conception. Purusha, nevertheless, exists even within the most unenlightened being. It may be unrealized, but it is nevertheless present and potential. In the Hindu view we are to see in each person not only his or her "caughtness," but this potential, essential (some even use the term "divine") self.

FOR REFLECTION AND DISCUSSION

1. Consider the concept of the "mind's eye." Can we experience it directly, the way we experience, say, an image, or a thought? If yes, what puzzle does that create? If no, how do we know there is a mind's eye?
2. Find a newspaper article or a historical event illustrating the thesis that belief systems can cause behavior that increases Dukkha. Explain how the item illustrates that thesis.
3. This chapter suggests that Purusha, a psychological component within each of us, contains the understanding of just what is enlightenment. Do you agree with this idea? If not, why not? If yes, then why are we not all enlightened? What is preventing it?

23

The Eight Angas, Part 1: The Practices

The preceding chapter described the mind before any enlightenment takes place. This and the next chapter describe the changes that must occur to bring the mind to the other extreme, to complete enlightenment. As with the Buddhist eight-fold path, in Yoga one also transforms the mind by following a variety of activities. These are collectively called the eight angas, or limbs, of Yoga. While not one-to-one with the Buddhist eight-fold path, the set is very similar.

The eight angas divide conveniently into two categories, the Practices and the Experiences. The four Practice angas are: Yama (attitudes toward the world), Niyama (attitudes toward oneself), Asana (postures), and Prana (breath). These four are presented in this chapter. The four Experience angas are presented in the next chapter.

In Yoga, we not only diminish the cravings but replace them with a set of ideals or "attitudes." These are characterized by the first two angas, the Yamas and the Niyamas. Each of these two angas prescribes several modes of relating to the world and to oneself, respectively.

THE FIVE YAMAS
(ATTITUDES TOWARD THE WORLD)

This first anga describes five attitudes that one should take toward the world, and especially toward other people. These attitudes are described here.

Harmlessness

This is the familiar *ahimsa* (see chap. 11; also Right Action in the eight-fold path). We are to strive to be harmless. Desikachar (1977) made the point that ahimsa is more positive than harmlessness alone. In our relationships with people we should strive to always show concern, consideration, good will, positive regard, to all others. In other words, ahimsa embraces the compassionate stance we discussed in chapter 11.

Truthfulness

This is the obvious ethical position that we must speak truly in our dealings with others (cf. Right Speech in the eight-fold path). Being truthful, however, defers to *ahimsa*. It is recognized that one may need to shade the truth in order to ameliorate or prevent the suffering of others. In a talk at Stony Brook University, Swami Satchidananda gave this example:

> Suppose I am sitting alone in the woods when a young woman appears, fearful and agitated, saying "Help me! A man has been following. He wants to kill me!" She then runs off into another part of the woods. A few minutes later a fierce-looking fellow holding a dagger appears saying "Did a woman pass by here?"

> I do not feel obligated, says Satchidananda, to tell this fellow the truth.

We can all think of examples: Do we not tactfully temper our criticism of another's performance? Do we tell a dying woman that her son was just killed in an accident? Compassion can be weightier than truthfulness. These examples, however, all describe consideration of others. We are not to stray from the truth for self-serving reasons.

Trustworthiness

Be trustworthy and dependable. Obligations undertaken are to be carried out as reliably as possible. This Yama overlaps with Right Livelihood in the Buddhist eight-fold path. It might be characterized as Right Dealings while gaining one's livelihood.

Chastity

This term is a translation from the Sanskrit term *Brahmacarya*, which is generally translated as celibacy. Desikachar (1977, p. 109), however, noted that this translation is off the mark, that such an ideal (celibacy) would conflict with the Hindu ideal of having a family. A closer translation is chastity, in the same sense that medieval European literature would describe a chaste wife or husband. They might enjoy appropriate sexual activity with each other, but beyond that they avoid irrelevant erotic stimulation, and turn away when it occurs. The aim is to subdue sexual restlessness.

Let me clarify this meaning with an example. Suppose I am strolling along pondering some philosophical or personal question. I happen to pass an advertisement, a poster showing a couple in an erotic pose. If I am aroused and snared by that arousal then the cravings are not adequately transformed. My inner life is vulnerable to irrelevant, externally evoked sensual disturbances. The attitude of Brahmacarya is not to eliminate sexuality, but to calm its craving.

Inner Focus

One should resist and turn away from the pull of worldly goods. It is like the concept of detachment, particularly with respect to worldly goods. One should learn to ignore their ubiquitous enticement. Wordsworth's "The world is too much with us, late and soon. Getting and spending we lay waste our powers" echoes this Yama. This Yama also directs us to cultivate our inner transformation. It is similar to the Buddhist Right Effort in the sense that our efforts are to be directed toward self-transformation rather than to "getting and spending."

THE FOUR NIYAMAS
(ATTITUDES TOWARD ONESELF)

This second anga, cultivation of the Niyamas, also stipulates ideal attitudes, but these are attitudes we take toward ourselves. Unlike the Yamas, which specify our relations to the world and to others, the Niyamas could be practiced if we were alone on a deserted island. There are several Niyamas but it suits our purpose to limit ourselves to four of these.

Purification

This first Niyama is concerned with our inner and outer well being. On the inner side, we want to monitor our mind and general state of being. This overlaps with the Buddhist Right Thoughts in the eight-fold path. We must become sensitive to thoughts that express anger, greed, (pejorative) judgments, and the like. Such thoughts should no longer be impulses to action, but should be treated as signals that something within needs to be changed. They signal that a craving (or anger or fear) needs to be dealt with, or a value (or bias or conception) needs to be questioned. Furthermore, mental restlessness is to be diminished. When immersion or concentration is difficult, when the mind seems to be going its own way, that is a signal to calm the mind. Meditation practice aimed at calming the mind is part of this Niyama.

Outer well-being, the other side of this Niyama, is a concern with one's health. The posture (asana) and breathing (prana) exercises are a testimonial to this concern. This also includes a healthful diet and abstention from harmful products such as tobacco and alcohol. Except for a greater stress on vegetarianism and less on aerobics, the yogis advocate a diet and exercise regimen similar to what we in the west would consider healthy. It is from a Yoga teacher that I first heard the statement that the body is the temple of the spirit and must be respected.

This emphasis on physical health is one of the few points in which Yoga differs from Buddhism. In my experience, Buddhism focuses entirely on inner process. We aim at escaping not illness but the suffering that illness produces, that is, our reaction to the illness. In all my readings in Buddhism, I have found no manual devoted to care of the body, no prescriptions for maintaining physical health. A few Buddhist monks I've questioned agree with my assessment of this literature. Among yogic writers, however, such prescriptions are commonplace. The attitude of the yogic authors seems to be: To attain serenity it is essential that we purify our minds, but it helps to be healthy.

Attain Right Views

This is identical to the Right Views branch of the Buddhist eight-fold path. Study the insights of enlightened teachers. Meditate on our psychological makeup and on the human condition. As with the Buddhist Right Views, we want to see clearly the truth about ourselves and others, and about the human condition.

Contentment

Develop an attitude of accommodation to the frustrations and irritations of life when they are inevitable and cannot be changed. Other Yoga authors speak of this Niyama as "equanimity," a sublime acceptance of the widest range of life's alternatives. This attitude of equanimity is another form of the Buddhist ideal of detachment. The Buddhists teach, don't be attached to winning, to comforts, to particular circumstances of life. Rather, be accepting of a wide-range of possibilities.

Of course, if disturbing conditions can be changed, change them. But if not, cultivate an attitude of contentment with what exists. We're experiencing a harsh winter? Do what you can to be comfortable, but after that, be indifferent. Accept, even be content with that which is unavoidable. I described an incident (chap. 21) where my daughter and I shoveled a car out of a snow bank at 2 a.m. We were both in the same objectively harsh circumstance but our attitudes, our state within this circumstance, sharply contrasted.

Devotion to Isvara

Here for the first time in this book that describes two religious systems, we introduce a god-like idea. Isvara refers to God but is different in conception from the common western sense of God. We in the West tend to think of God as an entity both all-powerful and loving. In times of trouble, therefore, we pray to God to lighten our burdens or to change the world around us so that our difficulties are removed. Thus, we might pray for the health of a loved one, or for the elimination of some danger. We relate to God in prayer much as a child might to a father. Indeed, our most common epithet is God the father. Isvara, however, is better characterized as God the guru. Isvara is conceived as the perfect enlightened being. In a platonic sense, Isvara is the essence of the wise, transformed, clear-seeing individual. The approach of the yogi to Isvara is different, therefore, from the western approach to God. One communes with Isvara to further one's progress along the path. When doubt, discouragement, or any psychological obstacle to progress on the path arises, one turns to Isvara. How would the perfect being overcome these obstacles? When one seeks strength in facing a difficult or fearful situation, one communes with Isvara. In short, one does not pray to Isvara in the western mode, since Isvara does not change the external world nor dispense its benefits. Rather, one communes with Isvara for inner change: for wisdom, and strength. Isvara is the model from whom we draw inspiration.

In Buddhism there is no comparable God. The Buddha, however, plays the role for Buddhists that Isvara does for yogis. I've heard Western religious leaders, ignorant of all but the most superficial aspects of Buddhism, dismiss the Buddhists as people who pray to idols. This, of course, is a misconception. The statues of the Buddha, many and famous throughout the East, are embodiments of the perfect teacher, the model of ideal behavior. The statue is a stimulus for communing with that fully enlightened being. A statue in not, per se, necessary. But the intense evocation of and meditation on the image of the Buddha is an aid to progress on the path, in the same way as is vividly imagining Isvara.

Isvara is also important in helping us relate to our daily tasks and obligations. An attitude is instilled that is similar to Thomas Merton's advice "Make a chair as though an angel were going to sit on it." The corresponding yogic prescription, part of this fourth Niyama, is: Perform your work as a gift to Isvara; work for the sake of the work and not for the sake of the goal. Perform all your obligations and chores with a sense of care, service, and ceremony, as though the finished product were intended for Isvara.

THE ASANAS AND PRANA
(POSTURES AND BREATH PRACTICES)

These two remaining Practice angas, posture (Asana) and breath (Prana) exercises, have been mentioned in earlier chapters. Both illustrate the yogic concern for health. Thus, the asanas serve to make our bodies stronger and more flexible. The Pranic breathing serves to dispel muscle tension, and to regulate the heart and blood pressure. They are also, however, the procedures to facilitate meditative practice. As described earlier, in performing the postures with breathing, we are practicing being in a focused, nonjudgmental state. This practice, if anything, is more crucial to yogic aims than the physical effects of the body. Consider our common image of a yogi in meditation, sitting cross-legged, hands resting on his thighs. This posture is simply another asana, called Padmasana (the lotus pose). Focusing on long, slow breaths during Padmasana helps induce the yogic state. Along with improving the body, then, the asana and pranic practices are congenial with the meditation experiences described in chapter 15 and in the next chapter.

We noted that Buddhism arose in India, in this Hindu-Yogic context. It was natural, therefore, for the early Buddhists to employ breathing and posture, particularly Padmasana, in their meditative practices. Slow mindful breathing while seated in Padmasana has been used by both Buddhist and Yoga practitioners down to the present day.

FOR REFLECTION AND DISCUSSION

1. "Truthfulness defers to ahimsa." Do you agree with this, or must you always be truthful? Give an example from your (or another's) life where being truthful and Ahimsa came into conflict. How did you (or they) resolve it?

2. Is it possible to *always* be harmless? What about the "bit-ter-pill," the life-saving medicine that has painful side effects? What other examples can you think of where knowingly hurting another person is unavoidable? In the light of such examples, give a more precise definition of ahimsa.

24

The Eight Angas, Part 2:
The Experiences

The remaining four angas are the Experiences. These four can all be subsumed under the single branch, Right Meditation of the Buddhist eightfold path. In chapter 15 we surveyed different types of meditation. Here the stages or depths of meditation are described.

Throughout the entire Yoga section, a central concept has been that of *immersion*. The concept was introduced in first discussing the postures and was then applied to different life examples (see especially chaps. 19 and 21). Meditation and the process of immersion are obviously intimately related. Asana practice, as I have suggested, is a formal method for practicing immersion. So, too, are the various meditations described in chapter 15. Whether one meditates on an image, a concept, or practices mindfulness meditation, one is to immerse oneself as deeply as possible into that activity.

The four stages of experience that are described here are applicable, then, when one sits in meditation or when one becomes immersed in any activity. These stages are:

DHARANA (THE TRANSITION)

This describes a transition state between commerce with the world and immersion in a particular situation. We have used as an example of immersion, the artist painting a picture, oblivious to everything else. The artist, however, first comes into the studio, finds the appropriate paints and materials, begins to paint, and gradually becomes involved in the painting. Similarly, the lecturer enters the room, greets the students, organizes his notes, then little by little becomes totally involved in the lecture. The changing psychological state during these preparatory activities is Dharana.

PRATYAHARA (NONDISTRACTION)

With deepening immersion there develops a diminution of the influence of the senses. Only selected stimuli come through to consciousness; the others are excluded. The artist who is totally involved in painting a picture is, of course, using her eyes, but is not distracted by sounds, hunger pangs, or other irrelevant stimuli.

DHYANA (IMMERSION PROPER)

This describes the condition that we commonly think of as immersion. In previous chapters we have seen a wide variety of examples. The artist immersed in painting, the inventor poring over his construction, the Buddhist monk meditating deeply on the nature of Dukkha, the yogi communing with Isvara, all are in this state. This state is not restricted to exalted ideas or high-level skills. It can take place washing dishes or brushing one's teeth. The Japanese Zen Buddhist, Suzuki, said that the Zen attitude is "When I eat I eat; when I sleep I sleep." When one is thus immersed there is no boredom, anxiety, angry thoughts, and so forth. There is, in short, no Dukkha. The aim, therefore, is to approach everything in life with this degree of focus.

We sometimes hear that the Eastern ideal is to "live in the moment." Without proper context, I find this phrase ambiguous. Does it suggest you shouldn't plan for the future? That would be odd. However, in the sense that it advocates being focused on your activity (even the activity of planning something) it is congenial with Dhyana. When one is immersed, one is not distracted by thoughts about the passage of time nor about the future praise this present activity may evoke.

Dhyana, of course, is at the heart of Buddhism as well as of Yoga. So much so, that when Buddhism came into China it was known as Dhyana Buddhism, which, in Chinese, became Chan Buddhism. When this movement spread to Japan it became Zen Buddhism. This movement, as I suggested earlier (see p. 76), emphasizes Right Meditation more than the other branches of the eight-fold path.

SAMADHI (ONENESS)

This describes the most extreme form of immersion. In Dhyana there is still mindfulness and a sense of contentment. One is aware of the process and of the satisfying feeling of this state. In Samadhi even mindfulness and contentment disappear. Of course, it is hard to capture these states in words (e.g., how do we describe serenity?) but writers commonly suggest that in Samadhi you become one with the activity. That phrase always evokes for me the image of the jazz saxophonist in a small nightclub playing an extended solo. His eyes are closed. Even in the instant that he feels a melodic passage his fingers are making it come forth. There is not a nanosecond between the music felt and the music heard. He has no thoughts, no awareness of the audience. He is, as even we in the west will say, one with the music.

In the west we tend to think of Samadhi as a spiritual state, and it certainly includes spiritual states. It is the state we attain when we are in deep meditation about Isvara or the Buddha, or in prayerful evocation of Jesus or God. As such, it is probably the most exalted condition to which we can attain. Nothing exists but a remarkable communion between you and this glorious, vividly imagined being.

Let us conclude these chapters on the eight angas by listing the important concepts and prescriptions. These are shown in Table 24.1

TABLE 24.1

A Comparison of Yogic and Buddhist Concepts

Yoga	Buddhism
The Yamas	
Harmlessness	Right Action; Compassion
Truthfulness	Right Speech
Trustworthiness	Right Livelihood; Right Action
Sexual restraint	The Third Noble Truth
Inner, not outer, focus	Rightly Directed Effort; Detachment
The Niyamas	
Inner well-being	The Third Noble Truth; Right Thoughts
Outer well-being (health)	———
Attain right views	Right Views
Contentment	Detachment
Isvara	The Buddha
Asanas and Prana	Meditation techniques
The Experiences (Dhyana, etc.)	Right Meditation; Right Mindfulness
Purusha	Buddha Nature

along with the corresponding ideas in Buddhism. While different language may be used, the similarity between the two systems is evident.

* * *

As suggested by many of my examples (the artist, the inventor, the musician), we in the West also value immersion. There is, however, a difference in emphasis between East and West. A European philosopher studied Zen Buddhism in Japan by studying archery (Herrigal, 1953). He apprenticed himself to a master archer. The teacher constantly insisted that, along with the proper physical stance, his pupils have the correct inner state, that they practice proper breathing and proper focus. This practice was performed for many months before any shooting at the target was permitted. Even when target shooting began, the correct inner state was stressed more than accuracy. Herrigal stated that this emphasis occurs also with training in other skilled activities such as the tea ceremony or swordsmanship. The teacher is always exhorting the pupil to value the state itself and to invoke or employ it in all of life's activities.

In training for high-level skill, we in the West also stress becoming immersed. "Keep your eye on the ball" we tell the tyro golfer. "Play from the heart; think musically;" we tell the young soloist. Nevertheless, there is a key difference. In the East, the state that one attains to when immersed, is of intrinsic value. The student is encouraged to savor that state and to generalize it to all aspects of living. The path to attainment is more emphasized than the outcome—hitting the target or performing beautifully. In the West, on the other hand, it is the outcome that is emphasized. We recognize the utility of focusing in the context of some skill, but we do not particularly encourage the performer to value that state or to generalize it to other activities. I have several acquaintances who are masters in some particular domain: poets, musicians, athletes. Within their domain they focus totally; outside of it they are like everyone else. In short, in the East the inner state is emphasized, perhaps more than the product, and the West the reverse is true: the emphasis is on the product.

FOR REFLECTION AND DISCUSSION

1. "When I eat, I eat." What do you think Suzuki meant by this? Would you say that the statement describes your approach to a meal? Why or why not?

2. Suppose you meet a man from another (non-Western) culture who has a pretty good knowledge of English. He says "I saw this word *serenity*. What does it mean?" What answer would you give?

3. An American businessman says "Everyday my life is filled with challenges. My job is to meet those challenges in the right way." What do you think he means by "the right way?" Answer this before reading on.

   Suppose you learn that the man had lived in a Buddhist monastery for several years and was still a practicing Buddhist. Would that change your answer? Explain.

25

Yogic Theory:
The Enlightened Mind

Chapter 22 contained the description, summarized in Fig. 22.1, of the pre- or un-enlightened mind. At that extreme, mental activity is dominated by the cravings and conditioned belief systems. These influence and distort the more anterior processes—planful thinking, creativity, and speech. Still deeper psychological processes, those of Purusha, are non-functional. There is no witnessing, reflecting on or transforming any of the mental activities. In the unenlightened mind these mental activities proceed uninspected and unquestioned.

Chapters 22 and 23 presented the methods of change, the eight angas. The first two angas, the Yamas and Niyamas, foster the development of a new set of attitudes. The other angas, the asanas, pranic practices, and meditation, help one attain to deeper levels of immersion. According to yogic theory, these various methods serve to calm and clear the mind, and to realize the complex of activities that we refer to as Purusha. These effects, which characterize the enlightened mind, are illustrated in Fig. 25.1.

As with Fig. 22.1, information is shown coming in from the left. It impacts now on a very different configuration. First, the passions (A

After

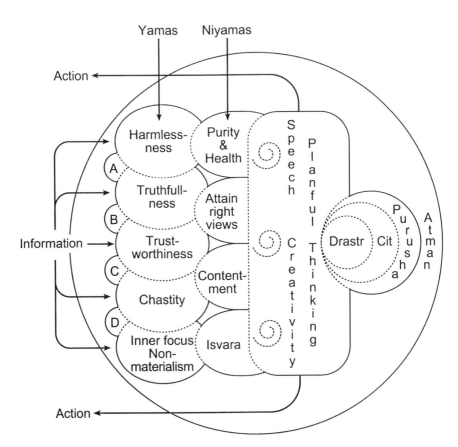

FIG. 25.1 The yogic conception of mind after it is enlightened. The passions (A through D) and conditioned beliefs are diminished, and are replaced by the Yamas and Niyamas. The anterior processes of Purusha are functional.

through D) are drastically reduced although not necessarily eliminated. They are reduced to the point where they no longer determine either inner pain, the mind's interpretations, or action. They nevertheless remain available for the mind's use. This is a subtle but important point. For example, in Part IV on anger, it is suggested that anger can have positive functions, so that anger may occur, but appropriately, with mindfulness. Similarly, we may feel grief at the loss of a loved one. The grief is genuine, but there is always a sense, deriving from that deep anterior place, of its appropriateness. Or consider ego needs. Partly out of a desire for fame a scientist may decide to devote his life to finding a cure for cancer. In such a case, the energy produced by that desire is well-directed. It functions in the service of a noble motive. The ego-needs, thus, can be useful. They are not so strong, however, that they overwhelm the attitude of truthfulness. In the interests of attaining fame the researcher does not plagiarize or distort the data. So, the passions are not lost although they are radically diminished. As I like to say: The passions no longer run the mind; the mind, instead, runs them.

The new attitudes, the Yamas and Niyamas, are now in place. It is primarily these, now, that receive the information and interpret it. These attitudes replace not only the energy of the cravings but the older belief systems as well. These older systems (beliefs, attitudes, values, and so forth) have also been searched out, assessed and, for the most part, eliminated. The new attitudes predominate. These are reviewed in the Yama and Niyama columns of Fig. 25.1.

Earlier beliefs may be maintained but with important differences from the unenlightened state. First, the beliefs have been inspected and, so to speak, selected. In contrast to your previous automatic, unthinking acceptance of these beliefs, you now feel that you have chosen to maintain them. Thus, you may decide to stay with the religion of your childhood. However, it would be with a better sense of its contribution to your life, and with a better understanding of its place in the community of world religions. Any arrogance ("My church is the only true church") would be gone. To take another example, you might choose to continue with patriotic beliefs. That is, you may appreciate the benefits of your country and work hard to improve the workings of your community and of your government. But again, arrogance, chauvinism, jingoism is gone. The beliefs that you choose to maintain are shown as the few small spirals in Fig. 25.1.

Except for these remaining few, the mind is clear. It is also calmed; it is no longer restless. Speech, creativity, and planful thoughts predominate. Also, the processes of Purusha are now linked to the rest of the mind. The full mind now sees and monitors itself, contemplates itself, and when necessary, changes itself. The essential self is revealed. The paradox of the (essential) self transforming the self has become a reality.

FOR REFLECTION AND DISCUSSION

1. In our quest for enlightenment we may give up our older conditioned values, our ingrained sense of right and wrong actions. Give an example, either from your own life or from the newspapers or from a film, where these unquestioned values produced unnecessary suffering. If we have given up these conditioned values how do we now know what are right and wrong actions? Try to spell out the new values.
2. While anger is certainly among the agitations and cravings to be diminished, the suggestion was made that anger might have certain advantages. What in your experience are the advantages?

Poetry Interlude No. 2

PRELUDE

Lord, I certainly know the rules:
Prayer for gain is the prayer of fools.
The law's the law; even if
The certified saint slips off a cliff,
He hurtles through unresponsive air
At 32 feet-per-second square
No matter how fervent and loud his prayer.

And words will never bring the rain
Nor add to the dwindling mound of grain.
But the cries you've heard, from the very start,
Are all those yearnings that change the heart.
Give wisdom, strength, ease my fear.
These, we know, you hear.

From *Look Down From Clouds* (Levine, 1997). Part 1 of a 2-part poem, Prelude and Prayer.

PART III

EXTENDED SUPPLEMENTS

26

Buddhism, Yoga, and Western Psychology

Throughout this book I have tried to show that Buddhism and Yoga (B&Y throughout this section) have certain parallels with contemporary psychology. For the most part, I've made these points by adding relevant *supplements* to the end of several chapters. These supplements were usually signaled by a row of three asterisks. Let me summarize the connections already noted between B&Y and Western psychology. Both:

1. are concerned with alleviating inner suffering (p. 6);
2. are humanistic and naturalistic (especially Buddhism), in that they focus on the human condition and interpret it in natural rather than religious terms;
3. see the human being as caught in a causal framework, in a matrix of forces. Among these forces are cravings or drives (pp. 29–33), produced by both our biology and our beliefs (p. 40);
4. teach the appropriateness of compassion, concern, and unconditional positive regard toward all beings (p. 51);
5. share the ideal of maturing and growth. This is interpreted in both East and west as greater self-possession, diminished cravings and agitations, less impulsivity, less "attachment," greater equanimity to loss (chap.12);

6. acknowledge that the mind functions both at a more superficial and at a deeper level. An anterior (deeper) part of ourselves can observe our own mental functioning, giving rise to metacognition, to monitoring of thoughts and emotions. A concept of the essential self is implicit in even the more behavioristic formulations (chap. 13).

In addition to the foregoing similarities, the congeniality of Eastern and Western views was seen in another form. Western researchers have comfortably incorporated Eastern techniques, particularly Dhyana (immersion) into their research programs. Several such programs have been welcomed and widely publicized. These include the work of Benson (1975, 1987) in the study of physical and psychological well-being, of Csikszentmihalyi (1990) in the study of creativity, and of Levine (1994) in the analysis of problem-solving. Also, Western research into the physiology of meditative states has been extensive (O'Connell & Alexander, 1994).

These several points of overlap were usually presented as individual supplements to the appropriate chapters. There are, however, more detailed similarities between B&Y and Western psychology that could not easily be presented in this way. These are larger aspects of psychotherapy and counseling. I felt that their resonance with B&Y would be better understood after the full presentation of B&Y. These next few chapters, therefore discuss other ways in which Western psychology overlaps or dovetails with B&Y.

Before focusing on the specifics of psychological methods, it is worth noting one other underlying similarity between B&Y and psychology. Not only are B&Y naturalistic but, like Western science, both are intrinsically empirical. Since many will find this a surprising assertion, I'll elaborate a bit. The term "empirical" refers to knowledge that is obtained about a particular domain in nature by closely studying that domain. Thus, astronomers patiently record the movements of the many bodies in the nighttime sky. Scientists studying chimpanzee behavior camp in the jungle for years observing the apes.

Also, empirical knowledge, knowledge derived from close observation, takes precedence over knowledge derived from any other source. No matter how eminent the speaker or how sacred the scriptural source, if their statements are contradicted by the observations, the statements are rejected. Observation takes precedence even over logic. Does your beautiful, logical theory predict a result different from that actually observed? The theory must be changed:

In what sense are B&Y empirical? Consider the following hypothetical scenario:

> A scientist is alone, the only human being, on an island. Being a scientist he is very curious about all the regularities he observes. Thus, he can study the planetary movements, plant growth, animal behavior, and so forth. He can even study human psychology. He observes, first, patterns in his own behavior: sleeping, eating, and so forth. More importantly he observes inner patterns: dreams appear at certain times, hunger comes and goes, thoughts appear in interesting sequences. He can observe his emotions, what evokes them, and what makes them disappear. He can study his states of happiness and of unhappiness, and can try to determine what produces these states. And just as this scientist attempts to exert control over the external domain of interest (change the soil in which a plant grows, domesticate an animal) so he explores the effectiveness of various interventions in this internal domain.

This internal domain, of course, is that focused on by B&Y. Here the B&Y "scientist" follows the canons of empiricism (close study, observations are paramount). It is a common assertion in Buddhism, both in the early literature and in contemporary writing, that the Buddha's teachings are not to be taken merely on faith. The student is to study for him or herself the truth of impermanence, that the cravings cause suffering, and so forth. Indeed, the dying Buddha's last words to the monks were: "Be a lamp unto yourselves. Strive toward the goal with diligence." The British scholar Rupert Gethin writes that Buddhism is a religion "whose truths are not accepted on the authority of scripture, but verified by direct experience" (Gethin, 1998, p 167). Thus, it is within this restricted inner domain, that B&Y are empirical.

FOR REFLECTION AND DISCUSSION

1. This chapter emphasizes the similarities between B&Y and Western psychology. In what ways are they different? How do

they differ in their concern about human suffering? How do they differ in their methods?

2. Yoga, I suggested, is different from Buddhism in its emphasis upon health (exercise, diet). How are they different in conception? To which view are you more sympathetic? Why? Which (if either) is closer to the western scientific world view?

27

Mindfulness
and Right Thoughts

The most traditional method of psychotherapy entails having the client speak. Early psychoanalysis had the person say whatever came to mind (free association). More generally, however, the client speaks of feelings and memories that seem related to his or her suffering. This method has revealed a valuable addition to B&Y teachings about cravings. Clients often fail to recognize within themselves subtle irritations, angers, fears, or sexual impulses. These unacknowledged agitations and cravings are frequently the source of the clients' symptoms such as anguish or compulsions. An important goal of this "talking cure" is for the client to perceive these subtle emotional states and to understand how they relate to his or her unhappiness.

It is almost as though this process is a preliminary to B&Y practice. The client, on this conception, is not fully prepared to "conquer the beasts within" (see p. 37) because not all of them are seen or felt. By helping clients to become aware of latent, unrealized agitations and needs, the therapist *prepares* them to better take on the B&Y task of self-transformation.

This insight arose from conversation I had with a psychoanalyst. We were discussing anger and I was describing the Buddhist conception, that anger is a source of suffering, that we are infi-

147

nitely malleable, and that we can confidently strive to transform anger in all its forms. I went on to describe some of the techniques for dealing with anger. She commented "You know, I can't use any of this with my clients. Their problem is to learn to feel their anger, to acknowledge and to label it." I thought to myself "Okay, When they have learned to do this, then they can be mindful of their anger and will be ready to get on the B&Y path."

This conception, that people lack awareness of crucial needs and emotions, was expanded in recent decades. Pioneers in a relatively new approach, Cognitive Therapy, added that people may also lack awareness of their attitudes and belief systems (see Bandura, 1986; Beck, 1970; Ellis, 1962; Ellis & Harper, 1975). People can have strange thoughts (cf. Wrong Thoughts) and are not aware about just how strange and destructive these thoughts are. For example, people might believe that everything they do must be perfect, or that no one must ever think badly of them. Any deviation from these automatic (and, therefore, unquestioned) beliefs causes intense anguish. Because this is anything but a perfect world, these people experience a great deal of unnecessary misery.

The clinical literature is, of course, filled with examples of clients coming to awareness of some critical thought or emotional state. The following is a particularly clear instance.

A graduate student was in deep anguish about how badly he was performing in graduate school. What was odd was that his school work, while not spectacular, was passable. He was not in danger of being dropped from the program and, if he persevered, would in all likelihood receive the PhD. He knew this and was, nevertheless, miserable about his poor performance.

He came from a warm and supportive family. Both parents were alive and he felt close to them. During the first few counseling sessions nothing dramatic was revealed, nor was his misery alleviated. After a school holiday, however, he related the following story.

"While I was home, I lost a pair of expensive gloves. My parents said nothing. If anything, they expressed sympathy. I was on the phone trying to locate the gloves, calling everyone I had seen. As I hung up the phone after one of these unsuccessful calls, a strange feeling flitted through my mind. I was envying a friend of mine. That puzzled me. Why would such an irrelevant feeling hit me at that moment? Then I realized, I was envying him because his father was dead! Even though my dad hadn't said a critical word to me, I couldn't stand the pain that he knew I had done something so foolish."

It was not hard for the student to understand now why mediocre school performance was the source of such anguish. He had this belief that he had to be perfect; this belief was connected to (what he thought was) his father's opinion. Also, he still harbored deep, childhood-derived angers toward his father. These insights visibly helped alleviate his unhappiness.

A particular "Wrong Thought" that Ellis (1962; Ellis & Harper, 1975) noted, and that has been widely cited in the literature, is what he calls *catastrophizing*. This is manifested in thoughts like "It's terrible!" "It's a catastrophe!" "I hate it!" when anything doesn't go right. A man's son paid $2 too much for a $20 game. The father's reaction was heated. "That's terrible! How could you be so stupid?" The father has blown the loss all out of proportion. He is in a state of Dukkha and, of course, is adding to the suffering of his son. Catastrophizing is the 180 degree opposite of the "don't judge" stance that is part of B&Y. The catastrophizers not only judge, but use language that amplifies their suffering. Phrases like "I hate it when . . . " or "That's terrible!" not only express the inner agitation but stimulate and increase it. You might check this out for yourself. The next time you find yourself thinking "I hate it when you do that," change your thought to "It bothers me when you do that." See whether that simple change doesn't lower your agitation.

Martin Seligman (1991) convincingly demonstrated how wrong thinking can contribute to suffering. Seligman describes an attitude of *pessimism,* where the pessimist responds to setbacks by thinking in universals ("This *always* happens to me"; "I *never* have any luck") or sweeping generalizations ("I'm no good at *anything*"; "*Nothing* will help"). Seligman analyzed the negative thoughts into three forms: permanence ("I'll *never* amount to anything"), pervasiveness ("*Everything* is always going wrong"), and personal indictment ("*I'm* a *terrible* mother").

Seligman, characterized the opposite kind of thinking as optimism. The optimistic thinker focuses on the particular situation, sees it as a problem to be dealt with, and is aware of the external contributions to the event. Consider, for example, a college sophomore receiving his first failing grade on an exam. A pessimistic response is: "I just cant do this work" (permanent); "I'm always doing a lousy job" (pervasive); "I'm not good enough for this school" (personal). By contrast, an optimistic response is: "This is the first time I've failed an exam" (limited in time), "I'll talk to the professor to find out what I can do to improve" (focused, solution-oriented); "I shouldn't have let Bill pull me away from studying last night" (externals considered).

Seligman demonstrated that pessimistic thinkers tend to be less successful in careers, and to be in poorer physical health. They are also more likely to become clinically depressed. As you might expect, his treatment for depression begins by helping the client become aware of his or her negative style of thought. Only by becoming aware can the client then start the work of changing from the wrong to the right habits of thinking.

In chapter 15 I described a set of meditations aimed at developing mindfulness of subtle inner changes. The method described in this chapter, the client speaking intimately to a sympathetic therapist, has a similar function. The client brings to light various hitherto unrealized patterns of emotions, beliefs, and habits of thought. With these deeper insights the client is now better prepared to be mindful of the subtle impulses and negative thoughts that occur in daily life. He or she is better able to work on the B&Y task of changing them.

FOR REFLECTION AND DISCUSSION

1. In the case history of the graduate student, what seems to be the client's wrong thoughts? How does this relate to the unhappiness that brought him to see a counselor?
2. Describe in detail one instance when you or someone close to you "catastrophized." If you do it habitually, what can you do to change?
3. Suppose a person close to you says something that makes you angry. Why is the thought "It bothers me when he says that," better than "I hate it when he says that!"
   Suppose you have the first reaction ("It bothers me"). What, according to Buddhist views, is the next step?

28

Problem Solving as Compassionate Action

About 30 years ago a new approach to helping people began to develop. This focused less on severe psychological disturbance and more on daily problems of living, especially as they arose in social situations. People came to therapists for assistance because they were intimidated and tongue-tied in difficult social situations. Others came because they erupted with anger and violence in certain situations. Both types felt that their emotions (fear and anger, respectively) were making themselves and others unhappy.

In response to this, psychologists proposed a mode of acting without fear on the one hand and without anger on the other. This brand of counseling goes under two headings: Problem-Solving Therapy (Christoff, K. A., et al., 1977) and Empathic Assertiveness Training (Lange & Jakubowski, 1976; Rakos, 1991) The fundamental recommendation is: Treat any difficult social (interpersonal) situation as a problem to be solved, by engaging the mind. The individual is trained to *take a problem-solving stance*. The thesis is that most of the time, we do not do this. We react only emotionally. Someone frustrates us and we lash out. Our boss is unfair, and we privately grumble. With

151

the problem-solving stance the client is taught to function from the more anterior parts of the mind, to consider strategies for resolving the situation. Examples and role-playing opportunities are presented to show the client how to react without emotions interfering.

Clearly, this problem-solving training relates to the B&Y aims of reducing cravings. Acting with diminished fear and anger (the goal of problem-solving training) approaches the B&Y ideal at its core. The proposal that we transform the cravings is, after all, the Third Noble Truth. This new type of counseling is so much in keeping with that aim of B&Y that it warrants extended treatment. In this chapter, I describe the problem-solving stance; in the next I present Empathic Assertiveness, a modern version of Right Speech.

To better understand this problem-solving approach, let us here consider some sample problems.

1. Mr. A, who dislikes smoke, takes a seat in a nonsmoking car of a train. A fellow comes in and sits down not far from Mr. A, and lights up a cigar.
2. George shares a dorm room with Bill, a fellow he likes. George, however, has one problem. George likes things to be neat; Bill never hangs up his clothing. The chairs and tables are littered with Bill's clothes.

Dominant feelings of fear or anger are generally signals that one is *not* taking the problem-solving stance. If Mr. A's impulse is to punch the cigar-smoker in the nose, or verbally abuse him, or yell at him sarcastically ("Hey, wiseguy. Can't you read? It says NO SMOKING") then he is not taking the problem-solving stance. If George grumbles to himself but doesn't want to "make a scene" or if he suddenly blows up and starts yelling at Bill, then he is not taking the problem-solving stance.

The question may occur to you "Why *not* insult the cigar-smoking fellow? Won't that solve the problem?" or "Maybe George *should* yell at his roommate. Isn't that what Bill deserves?"

There are two important answers to these questions. The first, discussed throughout this book, is the standard Eastern response. By becoming angry (or fearful) one's inner peace is disrupted. The unhappiness produced by the situation itself is compounded by the evoked agitation. The second answer relates to compassionate Right

Action. It requires that we look more deeply at what an interpersonal problem is.

Consider this analogy. A man goes to a doctor complaining of a bad pain in his back. A thorough investigation fails to reveal any physical cause. The doctor prescribes a drug to eliminate the pain, and it works. The pain is gone. The only trouble is that the drug has a side effect. It makes the man perpetually sleepy so that he can't function. Has the man's problem (the pain in the back) been solved? Yes. In an ideal way? Absolutely not. The solution the man wanted was to live his life in the normal way but without the pain. Getting rid of the pain, however, was accompanied by an unwanted side effect. Similarly, in interpersonal problem solving, we want to solve the problem at its focus—get rid of the specific pain—without producing any side effects.

Consider the two examples. The problem of the cigar smoker is solved if he stops smoking. It is not solved in an ideal way if he is hurt physically or humiliated. Those are irrelevant side effects. It is certainly not solved if, in response to Mr. A's insulting remark, the smoker embarrasses him by blowing smoke in his face, or returns the insult. These are surely unwanted side effects. Thus, the ideal solution is one in which the problem is solved (he stops smoking) with no side effects. Consider George's problem with his roommate. He doesn't want to live in a chronic state of complaints and hostility with his roommate. In fact, he likes Bill. He just wants the place to be a little neater.

The problem-solving stance is typically characterized in terms of "rights": In any given situation you and the other person have certain rights. Both of you have the right to be free of abuse and harassment. Both have the right to satisfy important needs. Both have rights defined by traditional understandings as well as by law. A problem arises when you feel your rights are being violated. With the problem-solving stance you try to correct that situation, *but with concern for the other person.* You don't particularly want to violate the other fellow's rights.

These, then, are the two reasons why fear and anger are undesirable extremes. First, they are states of agitation, of Dukkha. Second, they risk leading to wrong action: When we are unable to act because of fear then our rights are sacrificed; when we react with unthinking anger, then the other fellow's rights may be needlessly violated.

Actually, there is a third reason, also related to Right Action, why the problem-solving stance is preferable to reacting from raw emotions. Taking a problem-solving attitude permits you to expand the range of possible actions (solutions) that you may consider. In contrast, the emotions seem to narrow our focus to typically one type of solution. Fear makes us think that there is nothing to be done, that we're forced to live with a bad situation. Anger makes us think of punishing the other person (verbally if not physically), of threatening or seeking vengeance. In both cases a range of other possibilities are overlooked. When one takes a problem-solving stance the first step is to ask: What alternatives are available to me?

These alternatives generally fall into a few broad categories. Let us consider these in the context of another specific problem, that of a student, Walter, whose next-door dormitory neighbor, Jim, plays loud music in the middle of the night. Walter, a serious and hard working student, wants to sleep at night but frequently cannot because of the noise.

Here are some categories of solution alternatives:

1. Talking solutions. Walter could talk to his neighbor. Maybe that student doesn't realize that anyone is being disturbed. In the high school he came from all his friends lived as he does. Talking to the fellow means, of course, that Walter will be complaining about or criticizing him to his face. How one can criticize effectively is detailed in the next chapter.
2. Adjustment solutions: Walter might try sleeping with earplugs, or add insulation to the common wall, or change rooms. If none of these work, he can practice focusing his mind so that the noise is excluded.
3. Generosity solutions: Walter could offer to buy Jim a set of earphones, thus acknowledging his right to listen to loud music when he feels like it.
4. Pressure solutions: Walter could check with his dorm counselor or the college housing office on whether the fellow isn't breaking established rules. He can ask that the rules be enforced.
5. Punishment solutions: Walter could bang on his neighbor's door yelling "Cut out the noise, or else!" He could play his own stereo set loudly during the morning when he knows his neighbor is sleeping. Angry people tend to react this way first. Given our dis-

cussions of Ahimsa, of side effects, and of rights, it should be the *last* solution considered when nothing else works.

There are, clearly, more alternatives than brooding in silence or acting angrily. I have organized the list for Walter's problem according to how much trouble and possible side effects are involved. For any problem, I think, one can organize the alternatives along such a scale. Talking solutions are typically at the top, requiring the least trouble and risking the fewest side effects. Also, if done properly they produce the fairest results.

I once asked a friend whose wisdom I respect, what is her most important advice to young couples who are about to get married. "I tell them," she said, "that they should always try to talk with each other about their problems." Right Speech as a way of solving a problem is so valuable that the next chapter is devoted entirely to it.

FOR REFLECTION AND DISCUSSION

1. Five categories of solutions were described in this chapter. Consider Mr. A's problem with the cigar smoker. Apply each of the five categories of solution to Mr. A's problem. What might he do in each case to solve his problem? (For example, one adjustment solution might be for Mr. A to open his window. Can you think of another?) Similarly apply the five categories to George's problem with his roommate, Bill.
2. Did you find that some of the categories didn't apply? Are there other types of solutions besides these five that might be added?

29

Empathic Assertiveness as Right Speech

Usually, an interpersonal problem takes the form that, from your point of view, the other person is doing something wrong and is creating the problem for you. As we just discussed, talking with the other person is a useful first step. This solution, however, requires criticizing the other person. One of the concerns of assertiveness training is how to give criticism so that the problem is solved with minimal side effects.

When we criticize another person, our aim is to win his or her co-operation in bringing about the solution. How can we best evoke a cooperative attitude from the other person? Several principles have emerged and are routinely taught for achieving this. Let's review the most important of these principles.

1. Presenting Yourself. This concerns not what you say, but rather how you say it. The basic recommendations are: (a) Maintain good eye contact; look at the person in an informal conversational style; (b) Use a good voice; speak to be understood using an audible but not loud voice.

Avoid the two extremes. An overly timid approach involves look-ing away, as if fearing to face the other person, and mumbling or speaking too softly. An overly angry approach is overbearing, with frowning and scolding as though the other person were a trouble-some child. In empathic assertiveness, you appear confident and sympathetic, ready to stand up for your rights, without showing ill will toward the other fellow. The key words are eye contact and good voice.

2. I-Talk.   It has been noted by several authors that a blunt state-ment of the criticism, "telling it like it is" (e.g., George telling his roommate "You're such a slob!") is not apt to be effective. Blunt criti-cism has the sound of an attack. The person may then get his guard up, and become defensive or resentful. The likely result is that he at-tacks back or simply defends himself. The solving of the problem gets lost in the process.

How, then, does one effectively express one's displeasure? By de-scribing it. What you want to convey is just that, your unhappiness about the situation. Thus, George can say "I have to tell you, Bill, it bothers me to see clothing all over the place. We both work hard to keep the room clean yet it still looks like a mess. It's embarrassing when friends come over. Don't you think it would help if we each al-ways hung our things up?"

Walter, the student whose neighbor, Jim, plays music in the middle of the night, can say to the fellow: "I have a problem, Jim. The music coming from your room at night is so loud that I can't sleep. The walls seem to be paper thin." Walter could then suggest possible solutions (limit playing time, use earphones).

Notice certain features in these examples of how to present criti-cism: There are no insults. Instead of "You this" and "You that" it is "It bothers me," "I have a problem." No accusations are made; solutions are suggested.

While we cannot show the tone of voice or how eye contact is made, we do see another way to humanize the situation: George and Walter begin by using their friend's name. Among friends this is a nat-ural supplement to eye contact and good voice.

3. The Mary Poppins Rule.   This takes its name from a theme in the film *Mary Poppins* that was repeated again and again, and was even sung about: "A spoonful of sugar helps the medicine go down."

Ever since we were small children we have been taught when you want something, ask for it politely. Preface requests with "Please," or "Would you mind . . .," or "May I . . .". Why should we do that? Why is "May I please have that" better than "Give me that"? Both state the same message: You have something and I want it. Why is a person more likely to cooperate with the first form than with the second?

> I was in a movie theater recently. Although the film hadn't started, the theater was crowded. A fellow, Mr. A, was sitting in front of me with an empty seat on either side of himself. Another man, Mr. B, came walking down the aisle with his wife and said as he passed me, "There are two seats." He then went to Mr. A and said "Hey. Move over. We want to sit together." Mr. A visibly stiffened and said "I'm not moving."

Why did Mr. A react like that? Let's consider why he might not have felt like cooperating. It was noted in the previous chapter that, in any interpersonal problem situation, both people have, or feel that they have, certain traditional rights. Here, Mr. A may sit in an empty seat of his choosing; Mr. B may sit with his wife. An important step in getting another person to change is to see that offending person's rights, *and to acknowledge that he or she has those rights*. When you are polite, you are making precisely that acknowledgment. By talking in a command ("move over") Mr. B. said, in effect, "You have no rights. You must do as I say." Mr. A. then asserted his rights.

So, the Mary Poppins rule is as follows: To make your criticism most effective, make it more palatable. This, of course, is the function of those behaviors already considered: conversational style, I-talk, and now, polite language. The direct form of the Mary Poppins rule, however, is a compliment. The criticism might be prefaced with an honest, appropriate positive comment. Thus George, who in fact likes Bill, could start a discussion of the clothing problem with the following: "You know Bill, I really like you and I'm glad that we're roommates. I've got to tell you, though, I'm unhappy here. The place is cluttered; it's embarrassing. . . ."

I am not talking here about empty flattery. The positive expression should be appropriate to the relationship and to the situation. Frequently, however, the compliment, or statement of affection, is completely true but in the heat of indignation is overlooked.

4. Face-Saving Language. Because you want to win the other person's cooperation, begin by assuming that that person was not being malevolent, or insensitive. Assume, rather, that a mistake has been made or that there was a misunderstanding. Here are two examples (face-saving language in italics):

For the fellow who lights up a cigar in a no-smoking car: "Excuse me. *Perhaps you didn't see it,* but there is a sign that says No Smoking."

For the student whose neighbor plays a stereo in the middle of the night: *"You may not realize it,* but the walls are paper thin and the music comes through."

5. Keep It Light. This deals with the use of humor and wit in problem situations. It works best when the problem arises suddenly and does not have profound consequences. A light-hearted attitude can be useful in avoiding agitation.

> The chairperson of a large biology department gave her secretary, who was young and relatively new in the position, a set of documents. She informed her that the faculty would be coming by to read these and that it would be better if the papers did not circulate. The faculty had been asked to read them in the secretary's office. One of the senior professors came in later and requested the documents. He announced that he would be taking them to read in his office. The secretary resisted a bit and dutifully reminded him of the policy. The professor, starting to become impatient, insisted on taking them. The following exchange then took place:
>
> Secretary: "Will you be bringing them back?"
> Professor: (Clearly irritated, almost sneering) "No. I am going to throw them out."
> Secretary: (Brightly) "Good! You'll save us all a lot of work."

The professor, by his tone and facial expression, conveyed that the secretary's question was stupid. The secretary, instead of crumbling at the insult and suffering afterward, kept it light. By bantering, she deflected the insult.

6. Bypass.   This is a specialized principle for use when dealing with people in organizations. A clerk insists that some merchandise can't be refunded, or an airline check-in agent refuses to honor your already purchased ticket, insisting the flight is full. The recommendation is: Without anger, ask to speak to the next higher person in authority, to someone who can waive the rules. Keep going up the hierarchy until satisfaction is achieved or until all possibilities have been exhausted (for an example see p. 191).

* * *

These are the specific recommendations for Right Action and Right Speech as they are taught in contemporary psychology. This collection of specifics embodies another general technique for transforming emotions: When we have skills, strategies, or procedures that we can use, the emotions are much less likely to overwhelm us. Suppose that someone irritates or frustrates us. When we don't know what to do we are likely to be intimidated or to react angrily. By being practiced in the foregoing skills, however, and by having a strategy that we can employ, these emotional reactions are much reduced. Knowing how to take effective action, in other words, helps fulfill the aims of B&Y. It helps dispel fear and anger.

FOR REFLECTION AND DISCUSSION

1. You have a desk job. At a desk near yours is a coworker who is always whistling. The songs are pleasant enough but they distract you from working and sometimes get on your nerves. You decide to speak to the person about it. Using the recommendations from this chapter, what would you say?
2. Suppose your co-worker is uncooperative and is even a bit unpleasant about it. Now what can you do? (Hint: Remember back to chap. 28)
3. Compare Empathic Assertiveness to Right Speech (from the eight-fold path). How do they overlap? What are the differences? In particular, is there a difference in underlying attitude between the two?

Poetry Interlude No. 3

THE BEQUEST

An angel's hidden within me.
I've studied every thought, mood, sense.
No, there is no evidence.
But something keeps eluding me,
Like fragrances from memory:
The scent of sacramental wine
And smells of yellowed scrolls. I know
An angel's hidden within me.

"The shift toward the red," the astronomer said, "reveals that space at every place we look expands. It's empty. Empty space is all the tallest telescopes can see. Oh, here and there's a galaxy, but each recedes predictably. There's nothing mysterious, nothing free; no hint of any divinity. Just cosmic dust spreading relentlessly through vast, black space."

An angel's found within me.
It lies inside a speck of light;
Relies on me. Day and night
It drifts and waits.
But I don't know
The nourishment to make it grow.
I look for signs. What does it need?
How do I feed an angel,
The angel found within me?

"Inside the head," the biologist said, "are ten billion cells and nothing else. We study the brain thoroughly with electrodes and x-ray microscopes. Sorry to disappoint your hopes, but there's nothing mysterious, nothing free. A splendid machine is all we see, run on electrical energy. It's a machine that does calculus, writes, and sings. (Did you know that robots now do these things? They're based on circuits we found in the brain.)"

Behind the veil of daily life
On the far, dark side
A firefly blinked.
I had my first glimpse through
The glittering scrim.
In that instant the angel minutely grew.
Then I knew that wisdom
Was its bread and wine.
An angel smiles within me.

"God is dead," the philosopher said. "It's all explained historically. The threats of thunder, volcanoes, and death gave rise to myth. By well-known sociological laws, the myths become the essential cause of the creation of God. Belief and worship then arise, and persist. All based on myth. With radical change in the myth, god dies. This change, of course, our science supplies. The death was predicted; there's no surprise. (I can explain it again, if you like, with slides.)"

The angel says,
"It's true, the ancient God is dead.
But as He lay there, as He bled,
He saw the endless years ahead,
Saw empty centuries stretched ahead.
Saw countless daughters, countless sons
In countless Thebes and Babylons.
He gestured, whispered that his will,
Long untouched, should be unrolled.
He took a pen and mended then
His will; He scrawled a codicil.
To each of you He there bequeathed
A speck, a grain, an angel seed."

"The universe is dead and bare." The scholar justifies despair.
An angel winks within me.

From *Look Down From Clouds* (Levine, 1997)

PART IV

HANDLING ANGER

30

The Nature of Anger

Throughout this book, starting with the presentation of the Four Noble Truths, the emphasis has been on changing oneself. It is summed up in Fig. 25.1, where the "passions" (ego needs, angers, fears, and desires) are substantially reduced, and where the mind is cleared. Such changes, of course, are a tall order, requiring that we overcome the influences of biology, culture, and upbringing. Several techniques—attaining right views, practicing immersion, and so forth—were described, but in a rather general way. How do we make specific changes in specific cases? How do we apply the techniques to handling any one of the many states characterized as painful as Dukkha?

In this section, I illustrate the application of change to a particular subset of the passions—namely, to anger. I have selected anger for two reasons. First, it is much written about in Buddhism where it is considered a "poison," destructive of progress toward liberation. Second, anger has been a kind of hobby of mine. I have studied the topic in western psychological literature and have observed it in myself. The Buddha was once asked by a novice monk what he could do to diminish his anger. The Buddha replied: "Study within yourself the things that make anger come and that make the anger go away." This I

167

have done, noting the events that evoke anger in me and the techniques that dispel or even prevent the anger. These two considerations, the importance of anger in Buddhist teachings and my own experiences, have led to the present section. I also believe that if one learns to handle anger there will be generalization of that learning to other kinds of disturbance. Many of the emotions that arise out of interpersonal dealings (feeling stressed, intimidated, embarrassed) will be better handled.

By "anger" I mean the name of a category that embraces many states ranging from irritation to fury. These states all have certain properties in common, so that the general term may be usefully defined as follows:

Anger: An emotional state that is usually provoked, that is unpleasant, and produces the impulse to hurt (criticize, scold, attack) the provoking person (or animal, institution, or symbol).

Along with this straightforward description, we might add that the impulse to hurt can spread to hurting others. The man who is offended by his boss, for example, might that evening be harsh with his wife. In addition to being unpleasant, this emotional state has another disadvantage. It can take control of our actions so that we do or say things that we later regret.

I said that I am using the term *anger* as a category. Its range is suggested in Fig. 30.1, where I've organized many of the states into a two-dimensional space. At the left are the states of short duration, at the right are those of long duration. At the bottom are the milder states, at the top are the more intense states. To take some examples, feeling displeased is a mild state, usually of short duration. Hatred, on the other hand, is very intense and lasts a long time. Resentment is someplace in the middle both in intensity and duration[1]. For all of these I'll use the generic term *anger*.

Of course, there are other variables besides duration and intensity that determine the character of anger. Let us briefly review two of

---

[1]This chart, I confess, is not the result of any systematic survey, but reflects my own experience. If you feel that some of these concepts should be shifted in the space, that would be all right. I am simply embodying here, in a visible way, the fact that anger has a range of forms and that these vary in duration and intensity.

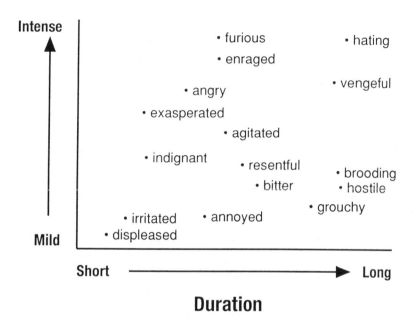

FIG. 30.1 The names of many psychological states subsumed here under the generic label "anger." The names are distributed according to the characteristic intensity and duration of the state.

these, the provoking conditions and the threshold determinants. A variety of conditions seem to provoke anger.

- Pain: A child accidentally hits you and you lash out at him or her.
- Frustration: A bureaucrat insists that a task, which you know is perfectly straightforward, can't be done. An assistant, despite your lucid explanation, does the work incorrectly.
- Disrespect: You're spoken to as if you are a child or an inferior. Closely related provocations are people scolding you, insulting you, commanding you.
- Injustice: One (yourself or another) is deprived of some good in a way that you perceive to be unfair.

Clearly, there are a variety of evoking sources, more than are contained in this list. We vary individually in our sensitivity to these various sources. Some people do not, as they say, suffer fools gladly; others are perfectly patient in explaining and re-explaining. Some people flare up at an insult; others have "thick skin," scarcely noticing the insult, and laughing it off. As the Buddha suggests, studying within yourself the things that make anger come, is an important preliminary step. In my own case, for example, I observed (over a few years) that I was most vulnerable to anger directed at me. I was patient with all kinds of frustrations. But when someone confronted me angrily, I immediately flared up. Having detected this, I have been able to work on eliminating this reflexive anger.

In addition to the different provoking conditions, another important variable is what I call the threshold for anger. The psychological concept of the threshold comes from the study of the senses where, if the energy is small enough, the sense organ won't respond. The ticking of a watch, for example, won't be heard until the watch has been brought close enough to the ear. At that point, the sound energy at the ear is strong enough to produce a perception. That minimum amount of required energy is the threshold. People with acute hearing are said to have a low threshold; people who are hard-of-hearing have a high threshold. Although the threshold concept was developed for the senses, a loose but useful analogy holds for the emotions and for anger, in particular. We may say that a thick-skinned person who readily brushes off insults has a high threshold to that kind of provocation. I had a low threshold to angry confrontation. When we're in an irritable mood we can be said to have a generally low anger threshold.

This threshold for anger, unlike that of the senses, is noticeably variable—some days we're touchy, other days nothing bothers us. It is useful to know the conditions that determine that variation. Within myself I find that the anger threshold is lowered by fatigue, a noisy environment, and alcohol. I've known people who have become irritable from a headache, physical exertion, or from having had a hard day at the office. Also, sub-threshold irritants tend to add to each other. The 3-year-old who gets out of his bed after bedtime doesn't bother you until he's done it a few times. Your response is mild, mild, mild, then bang! You're angry. Of course, the higher the threshold the less likely it is that you will flare up. It is important, therefore, to discover within ourselves the determinants of the threshold level. In some sense, our ultimate task in transforming ourselves is to raise the threshold to the point where no provocations evoke anger.

To summarize, then, anger is characterized as an unpleasant emotion ranging from irritation (brief and mild) to fury (prolonged and intense). It can be evoked by a variety of provocations and it varies in its "evokability," in its threshold.

FOR REFLECTION AND DISCUSSION

This section, Handling Anger, is derived from workshops that I have presented. Instead of suggesting topics for reflection and discussion at the end of each chapter, I am proposing a general exercise, to be carried through for at least one month.

The Buddha said "Study within yourself the things that make anger come and that make the anger go away." Start keeping a journal of your anger episodes. Every time you find yourself angry (ranging, remember, from irritation to fury) write down a description to the episode: When it occurred, what evoked it, the state you were in at the time (e.g., drunk, tired, headachy), and what ended your angry feelings. You want to determine:

1. conditions that lowered your threshold for anger;
2. provocations that were most likely to evoke anger;
3. how the feelings of anger ended;
4. techniques you brought to bear (a) to control your behavior, and/or (b) to dispel the angry feelings.

31

Anger: Assumptions and Levels of Expression

In this chapter I describe the various levels of anger-expression that we can have. This ranges from the lowest level—reflexive and unthinking—to total liberation. Before listing these levels, however, I want first to present the assumptions I am making in this study of anger.

Assumption 1: Anger Is Undesirable. It is, as the Buddha said, painful and profitless. Anger is undesirable for two reasons. First, it feels unpleasant. Irritation, grouchiness, losing your cool, are not good feelings. The mother who is exasperated with her child is in an unhappy state. These are clear examples of Dukkha that we're better off eliminating. Second, it almost always leads to the wrong action. I speak here from consistent personal experience. If I was angry I was too harsh with my child, or later regretted what I said to my wife. My own experience is also confirmed by examples from other people: The mother who says "I didn't mean to hurt the child, but I got carried away" or the person who, in an argument, becomes insulting.

This first assumption is pointedly illustrated in the following Zen-Buddhist tale:

A Samurai warrior, famous for his prowess and his haughtiness, came to a Zen monk and announced that he wanted the monk to teach him about heaven and hell. The monk replied "You stupid ox. Why would I want to have anything to do with a dumb, ignorant lout like you?" The warrior became enraged, drew his sword and charged toward the monk. Instead of cowering or cringing, however, the monk simply held up his hand. The unexpected response caused the warrior to pause, sword raised, his face contorted in fury. The monk said "Right now you are in hell." The warrior paused further. Realizing that he had just been taught a lesson, he sheathed his sword, and bowed to the monk. The monk then touched his shoulder saying "Now you are in heaven."

Having made this sweeping assessment about anger, I want to qualify it, to note that under special circumstances anger can have redeeming features. These benefits are described in the next part of this chapter, in the section on anger at different levels.

Assumption 2: We Are Remarkably Malleable.   Many people (Westerners) have said to me something like: "You want to get rid of anger? But anger has been bred into the nervous system over millions of years. How can you get rid of anger?" The Eastern view is that, that fact doesn't matter. We humans have also had bred into us an anterior system (cf. Purusha in its psychological aspect) capable of changing our mental and emotional processes. Such change, admittedly, is not easy. It requires not only commitment but self-knowledge and knowledge of techniques, and with all that it may take many years. Nevertheless, it is possible.

A few considerations support this assertion. Now and then we meet people who are sweet-tempered and imperturbable. Many monks and yogis have reputations for such evenness of temperament (see, e.g., the story of the Dalai Lama in chap. 2). And we have all had the experience of becoming more poised, less "flappable" as we have matured. The current assumption simply states that we can go far beyond that level of maturity (see chap. 12 on supermaturity). Also, consider sexuality. Its evolutionary ancestry is, if anything, deeper than that of anger. Yet, people occasionally choose to be celibate, and manage to diminish sexual restlessness.

Assumption 3: The Buddhist-Yogic Orientation Is Paramount.

Your primary concern must be to change yourself. This, of course, is a thesis underlying this entire book. When we're angry, however, we tend to forget that. In anger, the typical attitude is that the other guy is wrong, the other guy has to change. How many times have I heard people say "Of course, I'm angry. He did X and he did Y." The other person is made responsible for the anger. Contrast this with the attitude of "Thank you; you're my teacher" described in chapter 9. This attitude presupposes that you are trying to learn not to be angry. You thought that over the years you had discovered your vulnerable points and had eliminated them. But this person, this provoker, has revealed to you a couple of buttons you had missed. So "Thank you; you're my teacher." This commitment to transform anger takes priority.

A Yoga teacher related this anecdote:

> A young would-be Yoga master retired into isolation on a mountainside, growing his own food and practicing the various disciplines to attain liberation. After 10 years he felt he had achieved his aims and came down from the mountain. On approaching a nearby village, a boy who wasn't watching where he was running, ran smack into the yogi. The fellow reflexively became angry and hit the boy. He realized then that he had more work to do. The boy was his teacher!

Notice that the yogi doesn't "justify" his anger by complaining about the boy, that he should have watched where he was running. His concern is with his own inner condition. There is more work to do.

In summary, the three assumptions are: (a) anger is undesirable; (b) anger can be eliminated; and (c) this requires an emphasis on changing ourselves rather than focusing on the other. With these assumptions in mind, we may go on to consider the levels of anger expression.

To speak of levels is to remind ourselves that we are describing a path of self-transformation. You may accept the three assumptions, and may start working on yourself, but anger won't suddenly disappear. You change, rather, little by little. It is analogous to developing a complex skill. It doesn't happen all at once. In considering anger we start with the most basic patterns, then progress up to the most advanced.

Level 1: Anger Is Expressed Unselfconsciously to Any and All Provocations. A wealthy woman carps and complains continually. Her grown children avoid her. She can't keep servants. She scolds when they don't meet her standards, and they soon leave. She doesn't see any of this as her fault. From her point of view, the people around her are inadequate and to blame. This focus on the others keeps her from seeing herself. "What do you mean I'm grouchy? You see what they've done. How can you say I'm grouchy!"

Level 2: Through Socialization and, Perhaps, Intimidation, Anger Is Suppressed. It rarely appears. At this level, as with Level 1, it is also unacknowledged. One insists that one doesn't feel angry. The anger, however, has subtle effects. Because it is latent, the desire to lash out at the provoker can show up indirectly: as a practical joke, by sarcasm, by forgetting an engagement. Alternatively, there may be an occasional explosion of anger over something trivial.

Earlier (chap. 27) I described the psychoanalyst whose task with her clients was to help them label their anger, to acknowledge, and even to express it. Presumably, her clients were at this low of anger-expression.

Level 3: The Anger Is Felt, Acknowledged, Directly Expressible. Presumably, the psychoanalyst was trying to bring her clients to this next level. Now there is awareness of even minor irritation; there are occasional blow-ups, frequently followed by regrets. A glimmering exists at this level that there are better ways of handling things, Now, the possibilities of self-transformation are greater. If nothing else, the awareness provides even relatively naive people the greater possibility of self-control. They need not act reflexively from their anger. They can consciously suppress the anger. They can grit their teeth, so to speak, and say or do nothing. They can detect the beginning of irritation and can bring well-known techniques (e.g., counting to 10) to avoid full-blown anger. They can start to work toward a mature handling of anger.

Level 4: There Is No Anger.   This is the state of supermaturity. No reflexive angry feelings occur in provoking situations. Labeling and acknowledgment of anger are no longer an issue. Having, through the cultivation of mindfulness, become keenly sensitive to the subtle shadings of angry states, one is now confident that there is nothing left to be acknowledged.

I want to emphasize here that eliminating anger is not the same as eliminating action. We may no longer feel angry but we can still recognize when someone is unfair, hurtful, or otherwise provocative. Suppose a man insults us. We may puzzle over his behavior and try to clear up any misunderstanding. Suppose someone is dangerous to others. We try to stop him. As the Dalai Lama demonstrates (chap. 2), anger isn't required for action.

Level 5: Anger Is the Servant.   Eliminating anger is a remarkable accomplishment, and it would seem that there is nothing more to be done. Anger, however, may have certain benefits. Notably, it energizes us into action. It also vividly emphasizes to the provoker, especially coming from one who is rarely angry, that this particular provocation is intolerable. In this most advanced condition, we want to invoke these benefits when they are appropriate. Swami Satchidananda pithily characterized this advanced level in the following aphorism: "Carry anger in your pocket; take it out for times of injustice."

The benefits of anger needn't be given up in the quest for serenity. But rather than overwhelm and master us, anger now serves us. Nor is this anger, taken "out of the pocket," artificial. It is not a form of play-acting. Anger, rather, is like a seed that you may or may not permit to grow. At Level 4, where anger is completely gone, it simply never grows. Here, at Level 5, you permit it to grow occasionally, when that anterior part of yourself judges that it is appropriate.

Suppose you have told your 3-year-old son twice not to step off the curb without you. He runs into the street for a third time. This might be an appropriate occasion for taking anger out of the pocket, for letting it grow. You want to emphasize to the child that this particular rule is important. Your displeasure is felt and is made obvious, but there is always mindfulness. You don't lose control, saying or doing things you later regret. Repeating your instruction with a furrowed brow and stern voice might be sufficient. In general, the anger is real but measured; the action is appropriate to the situation.

At this highest level, therefore, anger is rare, but can occur when deemed appropriate. It differs from anger in the lower levels (1–3) in that it does not run you. Rather, you run it.

32

A Schematic, Physiological Model

Before starting the presentation of anger-transforming techniques, I want to describe briefly and schematically, the basic biology of anger. This knowledge will help us understand why the techniques work. Figure 32.1 is similar to figures found in most textbooks for introductory psychology. It shows two nervous systems, the central (CNS) and the autonomic (ANS) nervous systems. The CNS, consisting of the brain and spinal cord, is more familiar. The brain, of course, is associated with perception, thought, memory, and awareness. The ANS is a network attached to and surrounding the spinal cord. It carries out much of the automatic "housekeeping," controlling the heart, glands, and arteries.

The ANS works in two opposing directions. When we are relaxed it slows the heart and the breathing, facilitates digestion, redistributes blood (away from limbs and muscles). This relaxed state is called the parasympathetic function. When we are under stress, however, when we specifically are provoked into anger, the ANS acts in the opposite direction. It speeds up the heart and breathing, inhibits digestion, and sends blood to the limbs, preparing the body for action. This aroused state is called the sympathetic function.

Figure 32.1 shows the effects of a provoking stimulus. Of course, that stimulus is outside of ourselves and must be conveyed by the

senses to the brain. The brain interprets the incoming sense information as a provocation and sends a signal to the ANS that a challenge is
occurring. The ANS is never directly (i.e., without the mediation of
the brain) affected by external stimuli. The signal from the brain triggers the ANS into sympathetic function. Some of the resulting
changes in the body are listed in Fig. 32.1.

The list is really in two parts. Changes 1 through 5 are different
from Changes 6 and 7. Changes 1 through 5 are uniquely
ANS-driven. The brain cannot (except very indirectly) cause our pu-

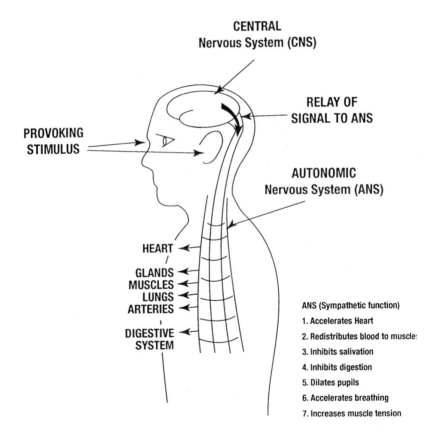

FIG. 32.1 A schematic diagram showing the basic reaction of
the CNS and the ANS to a provoking stimulus.

pils to dilate, our blood to redistribute, or our salivation to stop. The brain leaves Items 1 through 5 virtually entirely to the ANS. The last two items, however, are different. The brain, as well as the ANS, has some direct and immediate control over breathing—we can slow down or speed up our breathing voluntarily. Similarly, we can tense or relax our muscles at will. For these last two items on the list, in other words, there is overlap in CNS and ANS function.

This overlap suggests, in a general way, one form of control over the physiological conditions of anger. It suggests that by deep, slow breathing and by practicing relaxing the muscles, we might counteract the aroused ANS activity, and might even reverse it back to the relaxed state. In other words, it suggests that through slow breathing and muscle relaxation, we might calm ourselves in a provocative situation. Also, through regular practice of these two processes, we might even prevent an ANS (arousal) response to a provoking situation.

The brain also has a third link to the ANS, a particularly important source of control. A brief review of Fig. 32.1 should reveal to you what that is. The brain interprets the incoming stimulation as a provocation, and transmits this interpretation to the ANS. By changing the interpretation of the stimulus, therefore, one presumably should change the response of the ANS. This, of course, suggests that we should look for rationales and techniques for reinterpreting provocations. Such methods might reduce or eliminate anger.

One final aspect of ANS function not portrayed in Fig. 32.1 concerns its time course. Suppose the stimulus is brief (e.g., your spouse says something annoying) and it triggers the ANS into its arousal function (you feel your anger start to rise). If the incident is over, that is, if the stimulus is not repeated, then the ANS follows a time course of perhaps a minute or two during which it gradually returns to the relaxed state—you start to "cool off" and feel less angry. Of course, if you keep thinking and brooding about the incident then the brain is prolonging the signal to the ANS and you stay in the angry state. Without that recycling of the stimulus, however, the aroused ANS quickly returns to its relaxed condition.[1]

---

[1]Dr. Edward Katkin, a former president of the Society for Psychophysiological Research, informs me that following cessation of an arousing stimulus the return of the ANS to the resting (parasympathetic) state is rapid, a matter of minutes or even seconds. See also Chapter IV in Sternbach (1966).

33

General Methods for Decreasing Anger

We now consider techniques for handling anger. Let us begin with the most general methods suggested by Buddhism and Yoga. The following chapters will deal with more specific techniques for particular situations.

1. Among the general determinants of change, the most important is your own motivation. You must want to change. You must commit yourself whole-heartedly to the task of becoming less irritable and reactive, more light-hearted and imperturbable.

2. Also, you must adopt the orientation, that any time you are made angry, the problem is yours. Your dominant response should not be "You keep making me angry. It's your fault." Replace that response with "Why am I getting angry? What can I do about it?"

3. Take seriously the Buddhist recommendation to reduce attachments. The more we are attached to a specific state of affairs the more

we are vulnerable to frustration and, consequently, to anger. Broaden your notion of what is acceptable. The Buddha was invited to a feast (see p. 44), fine. The feast was canceled, that's acceptable. You get to see a widely acclaimed film, fine. You miss the film, that's acceptable. Neither alternative (doing or not doing) has added to the world's store of suffering. Another way of saying "reduce attachments" is "be flexible." People are frequently rigid about how events must proceed. Such lack of flexibility only increases the likelihood of frustration and, hence, of anger. Desikachar (1977, p. 42) wrote: "A little flexibility always reduces Dukkha." In particular, it reduces anger.

4. Come to know the yogic state, that state of immersion described in Part II. In such a state breathing is slow, an inner calmness prevails, thoughts of self, of time passing, of frustration do not exist. Practice being in this state at special "practice times," that is by meditating or doing Yoga. After experiencing the yogic state regularly, encourage yourselves to be in this calm, unhurried, undistracted condition as you go through life. This by itself counteracts anger. The text contains several examples, but here is another.

I normally bring my lunch to work, but this day I realize that I have forgotten it. I must go to the cafeteria to buy my lunch. The trouble is that the cafeteria is four blocks away. I can go there berating myself for being so stupid, muttering about wasting time and money, feeling annoyed at my wife for not noticing that I was empty-handed, and so forth. Or I can approach it as a walking "exercise," as a yogic activity. I breathe slowly as I start my walk, observe my breath, my footsteps, the world around me as I pass through; I savor the feelings, the scenes. I do, in other words, what Buddhists describe as a walking meditation. I soon find that there is no annoyance or resentment. I am simply taking a pleasant walk.

5. Come to know your own mind. We saw in chapter 15 that one of the types of meditations, mindfulness development, is a practice in becoming more introspective. You practice to become more aware of bodily changes, feelings, and thoughts. This can be done when alone or in social situations. Western psychology (chap. 27) also empha-

sizes the importance of coming to know even the most subtle and fleeting mental states. When experienced, these states are to be acknowledged without censorship or judgment.

As you become more sensitively introspective, you become better able (a) to pick up on body signals of anger, such as the clenched fist, the furrowed brow, muscle tension generally, (b) to be aware of anger patterns in your speech, such as sarcasm, put-downs, being hypercritical, and (c) to detect subtle, fleeting irritations and hostile thoughts. Being able to detect the earliest stirrings of irritation is particularly helpful. It is then easier to apply the techniques to reduce anger. If you are not aware of your growing anger until it is full blown, change is much more difficult.

6. Work to change your habits of reacting. As I suggested earlier, we vary individually in what provokes us. When you start to recognize your own particular vulnerabilities you can then work on changing yourself. I noted, for example, that I was especially vulnerable to angry confrontation. I dealt with that using a kind of meditation. I pictured my wife or a coworker approaching me angrily over some mistake they thought I had made. My automatic reaction would tend to be "You've got some nerve, talking to me like that!" In this mental scene I would replace this automatic response with something calmer, like "Before you get angry with me, let's check it out. I think there's been a misunderstanding," or "Perhaps I was wrong. Let's look into it." I would then practice (in imagination) these other ways of responding. I thus used imagery to form new habits. I gradually changed the habitual anger mode to this more dispassionate mode.[1]

Of course, I still slip occasionally. When I do, I later review that episode in my mind. I try to think of other ways that I might have handled that situation and, again, I practice that new way in my imagination.

---

[1]The effectiveness of establishing new habits by rehearsing the new behavior in imagination is well documented. For an introduction to this literature see Annett (1995).

7. Be realistic about the magnitude of the task. Recognize that it is like acquiring a new complex skill. Consider how long it takes to become fluent in a new language or to master a musical instrument. Transforming your anger is just as challenging. While the commitment to become free of anger is essential, it is not sufficient. It is like deciding that you want to be a concert pianist. Even if you have the most sincere, intense commitment, that is only the first step. Years of practice must follow. Similarly, even after affirming that you want to be more even-tempered and cheerful, years of patient work on your emotional responsiveness are still required. The Buddhists, remember, describe this as following a path. The goal may be distant but it is important to be on the path, to make progress.

*   *   *

These, then, are general anger-reducing methods. They are general in the sense that they will help in all kinds of anger-provoking situations. The next and final chapters deal with specific techniques for more specific conditions of provocation.

34

Specific Methods, Part 1: Right Views of Others

An important set of methods for reducing anger reactivity involves cognitive reinterpretation, that is, seeing others differently. We want to see those who provoke us within the framework of the Four Noble Truths. We want always to see how they are caught in the matrix of life's forces, to sense the interdependence that the Buddha stresses (see chap. 7), to see their helplessness (for want of a better word) when enmeshed in the world of Dukkha. This is part of Right Views.

We in the West offer a similar recommendation. When you are in a troublesome encounter with another person it is commonly suggested that you put yourself in that other person's shoes. Try to see the situation from his point of view. Try to sense that person's perceptions, his feelings, his state of mind. Try to understand, in short, the matrix of forces compelling that individual. You will be less angry and you will be in a better condition to deal fairly and effectively with the problem.

For an example of how right and wrong views influence our inner state, consider an exercise I have used at the beginning of workshops. I tell the participants:

I am going to read a scene to you. You might think of it as a scene in a film. I'll read part of the scene and I want you to write out the rest of it, to complete it. It goes as follows:

On a bright, sunny afternoon you are sitting in your car, stopped at a red light. Suddenly, Crash! A car has smashed into your car's rear-end. While you're jolted a bit, you are obviously not hurt. But you can just picture the damage to the trunk and fender of your car. You get out of your car and . . .

At this point, I stop reading and ask the members in the audience to write out the rest of this scenario. (You, the reader, might now imagine your own completion). Then I ask them to read what they've written.

Almost every one of the responses describes an angry confrontation. Most are verbal.

"What are you blind or something? It's broad daylight."

"Where'd you learn to drive, you stupid idiot."

An occasional response is physical. "His window was open, so I went up and punched him."

After the participants have read their responses I say, "Suppose the fellow in the car that smashed into you says, 'Hey, don't yell at me. I was sitting here just like you. The guy behind me hit into me pushing me into you.' Suddenly, you're not angry with this fellow. Why not? Because you see his helplessness. Now you go to the car behind his, your anger redirecting itself to that driver. But that fellow excitedly says: 'Did you see what happened? A baby ran out into the street. I had to swerve into this lane to avoid hitting him.' Hmmm. It's hard to be angry with this fellow. You look down the street and see two parents obviously upset holding their crying child. Who do you get angry at now?"

Once you see the interdependence of events, the tight causal continuum in which we're all caught, anger dissipates.

It is easier to see this caughtness, this ultimate helplessness, with children. Nevertheless, even with children, adults frequently fail to see it and, consequently, are frequently angry. Here are a couple of incidents I have witnessed.

An 8-year-old boy went out letting the screen door slam. His father called him back in and instructed him to close the screen door carefully, not to let it slam. The boy nodded soberly in agreement. The father then engaged his son in a short conversation, asking him where he was going, concluding with a reminder that he had to be back within the hour. After this intervening instruction, the boy went out and—you guessed it—absently let the door slam. Now the father became furious and started screaming at the boy.

Our concern, remember, is the father's anger. It is not only a source of his own misery, but adds to the boy's misery as well. What might the father have done to prevent this anger? Here the determinants acting on the child are transparent, although the father fails to see them. He fails to recognize the fragility of short-term memory, especially in children. After the instruction about the screen door, he interposed a conversation and a second lesson about the time to be back, making it likely that the child would forget the first lesson about the screen door.

A mother gets angry with her 8-year old son for accidentally spilling a glass of milk on the kitchen table. This parent, like the father just described, fails to see the most transparent forms of helplessness, and as a result experiences anger.

Those two examples are clearly of accidents. But suppose the child intentionally, on purpose (as we say), does something wrong: A boy bullies or lies or steals. It is still necessary to see the forces—the motivational or even biological determinants—acting on the child. We may not know just what these determinants are, but we know that they are there. Our proper stance is a problem-solving stance. What can we do to help this boy change his behavior? That view of the forces and that stance are extremely powerful in directing our emotions away from anger.

When the provoker is a child, it is relatively easy to have a sense of these determinants and to be free, therefore, of anger. Our thesis here is that Right Views has this effect of preventing anger, even with adults. When someone provokes us, there is always a reason. It may be in the provoker's innate limitations (as in stupidity and rigidity), in a perceived slight (real or unreal), in greed or jealousy. Whatever it is, the reason for the provocation is always there. Sometimes we can clearly see the reason, as when we see that there has been a misunderstanding. Sometimes the specific reasons are not so obvious. On having Right Views, we're like the clinical psychologist who understands that the client's insulting remarks derive from important antecedent conditions, without necessarily knowing what those conditions are.

This assertion, that having Right Views eliminates anger, is buttressed by the story of the Buddhist woman and the warrior king (see p. X) when she says, "How can I hate you? You only did what your Karma made you do."

Let us review some categories of provocations by adults that produce anger. We'll see how cognitive reinterpretation—Right Views—can help.

Stupidity

This is a common provoking source of anger. Consider these examples:

- A colleague of mine—a famous professor and poet—doesn't suffer fools gladly. For example, he becomes irritated if a student, failing to understand his lucid explanation, asks again essentially the same question.
- A bridge player makes an uninsightful play and his partner gets angry with him for doing something so stupid.
- A new salesman in a gift shop sells a set of salt-and-pepper shakers for $10 when they were $10 each. His boss gets indignant. "How could you do such a thing! I told you they were $10 each. Weren't you listening?"

Our concern in these three cases is with the irritation of the professor, the anger of the bridge partner, and the indignation of the boss. Dukkha here is manifest within each of them (although the suffering they inflict on the other is not trivial). It is relatively easy in these examples to demonstrate Right Views. No one wants to be stupid. It is as simple as that. We may safely assume that no one, at the moment of birth, said to God: "When I grow up, make me stupid." No one woke up in the morning saying "I'd like to be stupid today and to fail to understand things. Yes, that's a good idea." No one does these things. No one wants to be stupid.

If you find yourself becoming angry (irritated, annoyed, sarcastic) at one who fails to understand something, despite your brilliant guidance, remind yourself of their circumstance. Think of it as a problem. How can I be more helpful to this person? Perhaps, you will even decide that this problem is insoluble, or beyond your capability to solve. But anger is clearly inappropriate. When the interaction is seen in this light, the anger will be less likely to occur.

Rigidity

This is a provocation closely related to stupidity. The rigid clerk will insist that there is only one way to do things or that rules must be followed, even when there are clear and preferable alternatives.

Not long ago, I was in a bank in which I had about $4,000 in a regular savings account. I withdrew $400 and about an hour later came in to withdraw another $400. The clerk informed me that she could not comply with my second request. The bank's rule was that you could not withdraw twice in one day. I thought there must be some misunderstanding and reminded the clerk that I was talking about my own money. She said she was sorry, but that those were the rules.

Anyone who gets angry with the clerk in this situation is failing to see human helplessness in one of its more obvious forms. The clerk is caught in the system. She has a boss that she must answer to, and all flexibility has been taken out of her hands.

Invoking one of the Assertiveness Training recommendations (bypass strategy, see p. 161), I asked the clerk "Is there someone here who can waive the rules?" She directed me to the branch manager. However, he, too, was adamant about the rule. He gave "costs" as his reason.

Let me digress for a moment to consider the possible state of the bank manager. Rigidity is unlike stupidity in one sense. There is an odd blindness when people are rigid. They cannot see the unfairness in their inflexible adherence to arbitrary rules. They may even become indignant that their judgment or loyalty to their system is being challenged. Also, there may be a motivational force—ego needs—operating. Such a person may need to appear important, a need that is satisfied by exerting power over the others. Or there may be fear, as was probably the case with the clerk, that flexibility will be reprimanded by higher-ups. Seeing those intrinsic forces potentially at work kept me comfortable with the manager.

Continuing with the bypass strategy I asked him for the phone number for Customer Service, which he politely provided. Upon hearing my story, the woman at the other end instructed the manager to give me the money, which he promptly did. Problem solved!

All very pleasant—I never became angry. I never evoked defensive indignation in him. Needless to add, I soon afterward changed banks. In this episode, however, I never experienced the least bit of turmoil.

What if customer service had sided with the bank manager? I probably would have given up at that point, satisfied, however, that I had given the problem my best try.

This was an example of seeing the clerk and the bank manager in such a way that I didn't become angry. There are, however, two other lessons to be drawn from this humble example. The first is that when, in a frustrating situation, you have a strategy to employ (in this case, the bypass strategy) you are much less likely to become upset. The second is that you can further immunize yourself against anger by being realistic: Be aware that you will not always succeed. Problem-solving and assertiveness techniques provide excellent strategies for getting around your obstacle. Most of the time you will succeed. But, of course, not always.

Taking that realistic view at the outset helps prepare you emotionally for the occasional time that you may fail.

Personal Attacks

Part of seeing the other person properly is to understand that the person doesn't see you properly. Let me state this in an extreme form: any attack or insult directed toward you is never personal. The offender never sees you. He or she sees, instead, a distorted or limited conception of *you*. As you come to understand this you will be less likely to take these offenses personally.

A friend of mine, a psychoanalyst, revealed to me that he had not gotten on with his father. When he was an adolescent his father was always hostile toward him, and was occasionally gratuitously mean to him. He described a couple of spiteful acts by his father that were clearly unfair.

I remarked, "Your father wasn't seeing you, he was seeing someone else." My friend paused and became thoughtful. "You know" he said, "He always had a hate relationship with his brother. I think something about me reminded him of his brother." He later told me what a relief it was to think of his father in this way.

My friend's interpretation was psychoanalytic. This was much more specific than I had intended, but it nevertheless fit with what I had in mind. The man who is angry at you or who yells at you, doesn't see you but sees his own conception of you. Let me give a more personal example, an interaction when I was in sixth grade.

I was generally a good student, typically one of the best three or four in my class. The sixth grade teacher (whom I will call Miss Jones), however, saw me from the start as a troublemaker, scolded me several times in front of the class, and gave me barely passing grades at the first marking period.[1]

Miss Jones, I submit, did not see *me*, a confused, scared, bright 11-year-old, but saw her own conception, a fabrication of a stupid, energetic wise guy. In this sense, her reaction to me wasn't personal. In this example, in fact, it seems obvious that Miss Jones' view was distorted by some peculiar bias. Perhaps the psychoanalyst's type of explanation would be correct, that I had evoked in Miss Jones perceptions appropriate to someone in her past.

When I assert that the meanness and the insults are never personal, however, I intend something deeper. Suppose Miss Jones had, in fact, been dealing with a stupid, energetic wise guy. Miss Jones' anger at him, nevertheless, implied that she saw only part of him. She failed to see the forces acting on him, his helplessness in the grip of those forces. She would have failed to perceive, for example, the possible intimidation and pain that his swaggering may have functioned to hide.

---

[1]This was a bad beginning, although for me the story ended happily. Miss Jones disappeared and a substitute teacher took the class for the rest of the semester. I was never again singled out for punishment. In fact, two weeks after the new teacher came, she took me aside and said, "You've been undergraded. I'll correct that." From that point on my grades were normal.

Let me drive this point home with one more example. At your job you make a decision with the best of intentions, with the best available evidence, and it turns out to be costly. Your boss gets angry with you. "How could you do something so stupid?" Your boss is reacting to the decision itself and not to your way of arriving at it. He fails to put himself into your shoes, to see the considerations as they appeared to you when you made the decision. The correct answer is, of course, "It seemed right to me at the time." The boss's immediate anger and insult reveal that he fails to see this. He is angry only at his own limited view of you, at the decision you made. He fails to see the *complete you*, including the state of your mind at the time you made the decision. In this sense, it is not personal.

*   *   *

The point of this chapter, succinctly stated, is: If you see others more completely, more in the context of the forces at work, anger will diminish in your life. This thesis was beautifully exemplified in a letter printed recently in an advice column. The letter was so apt that I am concluding this chapter with excerpts. No comment is needed.

> I used to assume that a wealthy woman I knew slightly was an arrogant snob because she rarely spoke and never smiled. I also had the notion that the woman in the supermarket with the whining children was a lousy mother.
>
> Then one day, as I stood in line at the grocery store, I noticed that the clerk never smiled at the customers and ignored polite conversation. I was tempted to tell her what I thought of her sour attitude when the elderly woman in front of me took a different approach. She said, "Honey, you look like you're having a bad day." The clerk looked up with the saddest eyes I've ever seen and said, "My husband lost his job yesterday, and I just found out I'm pregnant!" The lady patted her hand and said, "Dear, things will work out."
>
> That incident made me realize that people usually aren't rude because they are mean and want to make my life miserable.

They are unpleasant because they have problems on their mind and a heavy heart. My entire outlook on life changed that day, and I am now much more compassionate.

This change in attitude has made those around me happier, but the greatest benefit is mine. I am less angry and more serene, and I like myself better than I used to.[2]

---

[2]Permission granted by Ann Landers and Creators Syndicate.

35

Specific Methods, Part 2: Changing One's Own Attitudes

We continue here to consider cognitive methods for eliminating anger. The preceding chapter dealt with reinterpreting the actions and motives of others. The present chapter is concerned with changes we can make about ourselves.

Question Belief Systems

The Buddha understood that our attitudes, beliefs, and values (what we will, for short, call belief systems) give rise to cravings and that these, like any other cravings, can be frustrating. This frustration can, of course, produce suffering. Most relevant to the current topic, this frustration can produce anger.

Examples abound, but a typical instance occurred in a television show that I saw. Before a live audience, a television host had, as guests, four interracial couples and was interviewing them about the problems they encountered. During an audience question period a man stood up and shouted repeatedly at the couples on the stage "You people are betraying your race!" Clearly a belief system was motivating this action. The anger produced by the contradiction to his belief system was obvious.

How could such a person become free of this anger? He would need to change his views. This could happen in a few ways. Someone he respects might persuade him to change, or he might come to have direct experience with interracial couples. Another alternative, the most important for present purposes, is that he might himself question his views: What does "betray one's race" mean? Who says (i.e., on what authority is it) that two people whose skin is differently shaded mustn't marry? What makes an action (e.g., interracial marriage) good or bad?

Consider another example. A young man surprises his family by announcing that he's marrying. It is someone from a different religion. In many families, the reaction would be one of upset, resentment, anger. Such a family member (say, the father) is reacting from a particular belief system. In order for the father to be accepting, his views would have to change. Again, this could come about passively, through getting to know the fiancée as an individual, or through discussions with a respected person (e.g., a leader in his religion) who has broader views. Most importantly, the father could change by questioning some of his beliefs. Why *must* someone follow the rule and marry a person of the same religion? What justifies angry rejection if that rule is not followed? By such a meditation, one can gradually broaden the bounds of one's beliefs and be more accepting of a greater variety of life events.

Sexuality is a source of beliefs and, consequently, of frustration and anger. When I was a teenager the attitude generally instilled was that a young woman should be a virgin when she married. Young men, furthermore, were to marry only virgins. This kind of belief, the frustration and the behavior it leads to, is captured in a verse from *Spoon River Anthology* by Edgar Lee Masters (1915, p.62). The voice in the poem is a woman's who had been raped as a child.

> . . . the story clung to me.
> But the man who married me, a widower of thirty-five,
> Was a newcomer and never heard it
> Till two years after we were married.

Then he considered himself cheated.
And the village agreed that I was not really a virgin.
Well, he deserted me . . .

Today we may regard such a belief as quaint. Sexuality, however, continues to generate odd beliefs. For example, beliefs about homosexuality (it is unnatural, it is a pathology, it is a danger to the human race) are accompanied by notoriously strong emotional reactions.

Race, religion, nationality, sexuality. The lesson is clear. It is important to become aware of the beliefs and values instilled by our particular culture. Only then can we recognize how, for better or for worse, they are determining our emotions and directing our actions.

Let us digress here for a moment to consider a set of questions that frequently arise at this point. We are proposing that to reduce anger you should inspect the attitudes, beliefs, and values that your particular culture has instilled in your mind. This examination, with the consequent broadening or even abandonment of your various belief systems, makes you less liable to frustration and, hence, to anger. The questions that arise are: Where do we stop? Do we fall into the limbo of cultural relativism where, because all beliefs are conditioned by our particular culture, nothing can be accepted? What ultimately can we believe?

Buddhism has a clear answer to these questions, positing two absolutely fundamental beliefs. First, Dukkha is universal. We are concerned with Dukkha, with all the forms (boredom, anguish, fury, etc.) that suffering can take, and with eliminating all unnecessary suffering. This is a bedrock value, an ultimate measure. It is against this value that our belief systems are to be judged. In two of the previous examples, marriage is reacted against angrily. But where is the suffering that this act produces? This is one ultimate standard against which we judge whether our values are arbitrarily conditioned or are authentic.

The second fundamental belief is that enlightenment (being on the path, making progress on the path, liberation) is absolutely valuable and good. Conversely, being deluded and subjugated is bad. Any beliefs and policies that move people from ignorance and helplessness toward enlightenment and liberation are desirable.

In questioning and inspecting the belief systems imposed by your culture you evaluate these beliefs by these two criteria: How do they relate to alleviating suffering? Do they dispel ignorance, that is, facilitate growth, enlightenment, liberation? The next time you find yourself indignant or repelled by another's actions, ask yourself whether those actions are violating these two bedrock principles. Or are you simply reacting from more arbitrary aspects of your beliefs?

Broaden Tolerances

The yogi author Desikachar (1977) has written "A little flexibility reduces Dukkha."

Specifically, flexibility reduces anger. If we have a rigid preconception—a fixed template—of how life should be, then we're letting ourselves in for frustration and anger. The father, for example, who believes that a boy should be a leader, tough and athletic, has such a template. If his son doesn't fit this preconception, is shy and bookish, then the father is frequently angry and miserable (and adds to his son's misery). Analogously, the mother who believes girls should be feminine, should love dolls, and wear frilly clothes, has such a template. She becomes exasperated with her tomboy daughter. My therapist colleagues tell me they occasionally see such parents who lug in their child, insisting that something is wrong with the child.

Broadening your tolerances—being flexible—is valuable in all facets of life.

Several years ago trains to New York City that ran beneath the Hudson River stopped operating for a few weeks. Ferries were employed to transport the commuters. This added about 15 minutes to the trip. Much resentment was expressed, except by my neighbor who remarked: "I don't know why people are complaining. Me, I love riding the ferry."

In the section on Yoga, we saw that the concept of immersion implies that you take life where you find it (see chap. 21). There is a relevant Italian saying: Que sera sera. Take life as it comes. Develop this nonjudgmental, accepting attitude toward the great variety of forms that life can take. There will be less irritation, resentment, anger.

Know What Counts

Many of our complaints are about passing trivialities that do not really cause suffering. To paraphrase an old saying: We complain about a mountain when it is only a molehill. The attitude of catastrophizing (see chap. 27), of treating minor frustrations as calamities, is the exact opposite of the attitude described here, of knowing what matters.

An example of learning what really counts is seen in the following sad confession:

> My husband was a good man but we used to fight about one thing. He had a habit that I just couldn't tolerate. He would remove his shoes and socks and put his feet on the coffee table. Even people visiting didn't stop him. Many's the tear I bitterly shed over this. He died 2 years ago. I look back now and I can't imagine what was the matter with me. If he were here now, I would myself lovingly undress his feet and prop them up.

Another example comes from my graduate-school days. It took place in the late 1940s when, at the school, were several Europeans. They were typically people in their 30s, or 40s who were rebuilding their lives after the radical disruptions of World War II.

A fellow student, Edgar, was from Czechoslovakia, which had been occupied by the Nazis during the entire war. Although he had never been interned in a concentration camp, he had been impressed into slave labor. He was required to work long hours per day for a pittance in a factory near his home. Life, he said, was precarious. Food and medicines were in short supply. Worst of all, people would disappear. Those who asked questions about them also disappeared.

After the war, he came to America. Here he finished college and was now in graduate school. Toward the end of the first semester, as final exams loomed, we were all frazzled and edgy. The anger threshold was very palpably low in all of us. All of us, that is, except Edgar, who was as relaxed and affable as at any other time in the semester. When I remarked to him my observation about his relative calm, his answer was: "For years I didn't know whether I would live or die the next day. Having gone through that, I'm not bothered by exams."

This same sense of knowing what truly matters is expressed in an anecdote I've heard about the novelist Isaac Bashevis Singer.

When he was first trying to become established as a writer in America, his agent called with wonderful news. "The *New Yorker* magazine wants to publish the three stories of yours that I sent them. They insist on all three. Is that Okay?" Mr. Singer replied that perhaps not. One of the stories was already in press with a literary journal. The agent was thunderstruck. "Mr. Singer," he cried "that's terrible." Isaac Bashevis Singer replied. "No, it's not terrible. Little children won't die from this."

The poet David Axelrod has a relevant poem, "He Lists His Complaints," in his book *Resurrections* (1989, p. 46). The poem contains a pithy portrait of a woman whose sense of what matters is askew:

> . . . I wake to find you
> in the bedroom looking for a lost
> sock, a panic in your eyes I would
> reserve for cancer or a stroke.[1]

Another author, Richard Carlson, whose writings are congenial with the point of view taken here, cites Wayne Dyer's prescriptions (Carlson, 1997): "Rule (1): Don't sweat the small stuff; Rule (2); It's all small stuff."

EXPECT LITTLE (AND GIVE MUCH)

Do not expect people to be perfect. Errors will be made, accidents will happen, emotions will get out of hand, beliefs and lifestyles will occasionally be out of the ordinary. People will sometimes be greedy, and sometimes favor themselves unfairly. This, to me, is the character of life. It is filled with glitches and imperfections. As a result of seeing life in this way, I am much less upset by mistakes, accidents, or inappropriate decisions. I may take action to correct the mistake or to persuade the person about (what I think is) the error of his decision.

---

[1]"He lists his complaints" first appeared in *Resurrections* (Naşa Kniga, Skopia, Macedonia) bilingually while Dr. Axelrod was Fulbright Poet in Residence in Yugoslavia.

But I rarely get upset or angry over these faux pas and foibles. That's just the way people are.

Beware of the attitude that people owe you anything. In the advice columns is an occasional letter from someone who complains: "My gift wasn't acknowledged; I never received a thank-you card." The letter-writer's expectations have clearly been frustrated. Reduce the expectation and you reduce the frustration. If a friend doesn't call, or forgets a birthday (or whatever), it needn't be a source of annoyance.

The Expect Little rule doesn't mean that I ignore inappropriate behavior. I might speak to the person about the perceived neglect at some future time, but I'm rarely upset. Of course, I try to honor my social commitments, acknowledging gifts and birthdays. That is part of Giving Much. But I'm not hurt if others do not live up to this same exalted standard.

Just as the anger in our lives is decreased by expecting little it is also decreased by giving much. This particularly applies in a marriage (or other kind of partnership) where you and your mate agree to share everything in an equitable way: the work, the expenses, whose car is used. In such a situation, I will make a silent vow to myself—I'll give 60%. It's wonderful how this eliminates arguments. If I perceive a small departure from the 50–50 I don't feel "cheated." The difference is typically well within the agreement as I have interpreted it.

Three great benefits follow from this attitude. The first was just mentioned. There is less annoyance, less of the feeling that I'm being taken advantage of. The second benefit appears when there is ambiguity. Is cooking (her job) more or less work than doing the dishes (mine)? Is doing laundry (hers) more or less work than attending to trash and garbage (mine)? Cleaning the windows more or less than doing house repairs? And so on. Of course, there is no easy yardstick here. Nevertheless, when I was first married and believed we should do everything "50–50", I occasionally found myself irritated that I was doing "too much work around here." I complained about it to my wife. That, of course, led to an argument. Then we agreed to sit down and compare the work each of us was contributing. I was amazed at all the tasks she was doing. I hadn't realized. She too had been harboring resentments. I saw that there is a curious illusion in these unmeasurable activities. Your chores loom larger than your spouse's chores.

That is when I instituted the 60–40 rule. I wouldn't complain unless I felt I was doing *substantially* more than my share.

A third benefit of this rule is that when real inequality occurs—we're using my car much more than half the time—it's easier to make the case without argument or hard feelings. It's easier for my wife see the disparity.

Take a Problem-Solving Stance

This is a recommendation from contemporary psychology that was extensively discussed in chapters 28 and 29. Essentially, you want to see a provocation not as a cause for anger but as a problem to be solved. This shift in outlook is easiest when the source of unhappiness is a repeated pattern. For example, a student's sleep is disturbed each morning because his early-rising roommate is noisy; a wife is frequently criticized by her husband in front of others. In such cases the provocation to anger happens not suddenly at one single time but repeatedly. The pattern provides you with the time to go from being angry to seeing the situation as a problem. You have time to review your options, and to select the best approach. Most importantly, a pattern gives you time to rehearse how you will approach the offender, how you will handle his or her possible reactions (for the details of procedure see chapters 28 and 29).

36

Specific Methods, Part 3: When Anger Occurs

The preceding chapters dealt primarily with three cognitive methods for handling anger: learn to see the other person differently, question your own belief systems, and take a problem-solving stance. These methods can be practiced even in the absence of someone provoking us. Like other methods described—being in the yogic state, being mindful, reducing attachments—these can all be practiced when life is calm and without challenges. Essentially, we are trying to better understand ourselves and others. This can come about through reading, meditating, and reflecting upon our experiences.

In the present chapter we consider what to do when you are in the situation itself, when you are being provoked. Someone offends you and wrath is starting to rise. What can be done? A preliminary recommendation is: Learn to be mindful. Learn to be keenly sensitive to your inner state. It is much easier to deal with your own anger when it is just beginning than when it has taken over your behavior. Thus, learn to be aware of your feelings, of the subtle beginnings of irritation, displeasure, annoyance. Become sensitive to physical changes, to your clenched fists, your furrowed brow, to general muscle tension. Be aware of your own hostile speech: sarcasm and put-downs.

Phrases like "Are you for real?" "That's a lot of nonsense!" even if said with a smile, should trigger recognition of the irritation you're feeling. Ideally, when you find yourself merely thinking such phrases, that is the time to intervene with yourself.

Suppose we do detect these stirrings. Or suppose strong anger is welling up. What techniques are available on the spot? Of course, the cognitive methods described in the preceding chapters are still relevant. This purely cognitive activity, however, has to be performed quickly—you are smack in the situation. It may feel as if you are scrambling to change. Nevertheless, it helps.

One particular type of cognitive activity, specifically to be invoked in the provoking situation, is worthy of mention. Novaco (1975), a behavior therapist working with people for whom anger was a problem, trained them to replace negative thoughts with *positive self-statements* (a Behavioristic euphemism for Right Thoughts). Examples of such statements are: "Stay calm; just continue to relax." "Let's try a cooperative approach; maybe we're both right." "Don't get all bent out of shape; just think of what to do here." Novaco found that such training reduced ones anger in confrontational situations and yielded better coping behavior.

In the situation itself, the physical techniques, based upon the biology as we discussed it in chapter 32, become very important. The primary technique, hallowed throughout the ages, is to let time pass before speaking or acting. We described how a provocation arouses the ANS into the stress mode. If the provocation is brief then the ANS soon returns to the relaxed state. The concomitant feeling of anger ebbs. How long the ANS takes to return to the relaxed state depends on two main considerations. First, how intense is the provocation? Is it merely irritating, or is it infuriating? The former may require a few seconds, the latter several minutes for the ANS to return to its relaxed state. Second, and most important, what is your brain doing, that is, what are you thinking, during this post-provocation interval? If you are brooding about the provocation, playing it over and over again in your mind, then you are repeatedly sending a stress signal to the ANS. It stays active and you stay angry.

Thus, we are told to count to 10 before acting. Taken literally, this counting has two benefits. First, of course, it forces you to put a time interval between the provocation and your response. This permits the anger-state to diminish. Second, the act of counting distracts you from thinking about, perseverating on, the provocation that just happened. The stress state of the ANS and, consequently, your anger is not maintained by the stimulus of your thoughts. Once the anger decreases we are better able to take the problem-solving stance and to consider alternative solutions.

This benefit of a time period between provocation and response is clearly seen in the following example. It was communicated to me by a reader of an essay I had written (Levine, 1994) on the problem-solving stance.

> One Sunday morning I was awakened at about half-past seven by the steady whine of a motor. The sound came from outside, but it was summer, and the windows were open; the noise was like a coffee grinder rasping right next to my bed. I stumbled to the window and saw my neighbor—new, I scarcely knew him—vacuuming his boat! I was furious. Where did he get off . . . ? Half past seven on a Sunday morning . . . ? I would tell him a thing or two! Of course, I had to dress first and I had to wash up. The passage of time smoothed my indignation. I began to take on the problem-solving stance. Pouring myself a glass of juice I thought about how to approach him. I was now wide awake. Although I would have preferred sleeping another hour there was no longer anything to be done about that. My concern should be with the future, that he doesn't do this again. Also, he's my neighbor. I didn't want what you call side effects: bad relations between us through the coming months. Feeling much better, I went out and greeted him pleasantly, exchanging comments about the weather and his boat. Then I said, "Bob, I have to tell you, the vacuum-cleaner noise goes directly from your boat into my room. It woke me up this morning." Bob said, "I'm sorry. I didn't realize. It won't happen again." That was a year ago, and it never did. Of equal importance, Bob and I are cordial neighbors.

Note in this example the effects of the passage of time and how it permitted taking on the problem-solving stance. The writer was then able to be friendly, and to describe the problem objectively, without anger or accusation.

The passage of time, then, provides the essential framework for eliminating anger. Along with that, it is important to distract yourself, to avoid obsessing over the provocation. Engage in some other activity—count to 10, whistle or sing, or think about one of your hobbies – during that interval. Such activities block the unwanted thoughts, and permit the ANS to return to its resting state.

Activities that are particularly powerful in blocking those thoughts are deep, slow breathing and muscle relaxing. This is to be done in yogic style, that is, with full attention. By focusing on deep breathing and on relaxing individual muscles (your face, your fists, etc.) you are, of course, distracting yourself. But what is of equal importance, is that you are reversing the arousal condition of the ANS and helping to push it back to a relaxed state. By breathing and muscle relaxation, you speed up the return to that state. Over the years I have used this technique a number of times. The most vivid for me, however, is the first time I used it. Yoga was then relatively new to me. I had been practicing just a few weeks.

This particular evening I had to return to my university for a meeting with some distinguished visitors. Just as I started to leave the house, my 8-year-old son did something that infuriated me. I started yelling at him but he ran away and I had to leave. I stomped out of the house and took off in my car for the university. I spent the entire 10-minute trip compulsively grumbling over that scene, the scoldings I should have given, my resentments (who does he think he is?). When I parked the car near the building I was literally trembling with anger. I thought, "I can't go in to the meeting like this." Sitting in the car I took a few slow deep breaths, raising and lowering my shoulders with each breath, focusing on relaxing my face, legs, and hands. After doing these breaths for no more than 2, 3 minutes, my inner state was totally changed. I was now perfectly calm. The very memory of this incident was no longer present. I knew that I could recover it if I tried but wisely did not try. I, instead, anticipated the events of the meeting. The next day I was able to talk in an appropriate way to my son.

To summarize, when you feel anger start to arise, avoid responding immediately to the provocation. Give yourself time to let the ANS return to its relaxed state. During that time distract yourself from resentful, brooding thoughts; use slow breathing and focused muscle relaxing to facilitate the return of the ANS to the relaxed state. When you are back in that state it is much easier to use the cognitive methods, to see your situation as a problem and to weigh alternative solutions. Proceed with a solution when you are calm. You are much less likely to do or say things you later regret.

Waiting before acting provides, for certain kinds of problems, one additional advantage. You can imagine yourself talking with the offender when you are both calm and you can rehearse the scene. Picture yourself describing your problem in a nonaccusatory manner, using the methods of Empathic Assertiveness (chap. 29). Picture the possible reactions by that person (e.g., defensiveness). Imagine how you would handle them, always with the thought that you want to win that person's cooperation in helping you solve your problem. It is as though you are practicing a new habit of talking objectively about a problem. By repeated rehearsal you strengthen that habit. At the same time, the habit of speaking angrily gets weaker.

Let's consider a final example, and use it to review the problem-solving stance.

A young woman, a schoolteacher, married a salesman in September. During the school year they both arose at the same time each weekday morning to go off to their respective jobs. When summer came, however, the woman was able to sleep later, although her husband continued to rise for work at the usual early hour. To the wife's unhappiness, the husband was noisy as ever in the morning. He walked heavily, he sang while he shaved, he turned on the TV in the room next to the bedroom of their small apartment. The wife would lie in bed irritated every morning. Her impulse was to go to him and scold "You're so inconsiderate. Here I am trying to sleep and you're making the noise of an elephant! Didn't your folks ever teach you to be quiet when people are sleeping?" So far she had been able to suppress her anger and had not said these things. She felt, however, that she would explode any morning. She was afraid of a scene and an argument, but one of these mornings. . . .

What advice can we give this young woman?

1. Do not deal with this problem in the morning when the ANS is aroused. Notice how the imagined anger outburst consists of insults. Long-range side effects might indeed follow.
2. Do not brood and grumble to yourself about the situation. By distraction, by focusing on breathing and relaxing, change from the angry state.
3. When he is out of the house and you have calmed down, take a problem-solving stance. Here are two types of solutions that you might consider.

    (a) Right-Speech Solutions: Talk to your husband at a pleasant, quiet time and describe your problem. The approach should be conversational and friendly. The attitude should be "I have a problem," rather than "You're doing something wrong." Rehearse in imagination how you think the conversation will go. If you imagine yourself becoming accusatory or righteously indignant, find other ways to present your case. Rehearse it a few times. In that way you strengthen the habit of talking cordially about problems.

    (b) Adjustment Solutions: Get up with your husband, have breakfast with him, and return to sleep after he leaves; sleep with ear-plugs.

How does one decide which solution to employ? Much depends on individual preferences. If you enjoy your husband's company sufficiently and can easily go back to sleep you might be happy with the first alternative under (b). If, on the other hand, you resent having to "give in," feel that it is unfair, then speaking to him should be considered.

*   *   *

These then are the chief recommendations when anger starts to well up. Give yourself time before acting, try to get into the yogic state, and acquire the habit of speaking about your problems in a comfortable, conversational style. If you practice these and the cognitive methods described in the preceding chapters, then an actual provocation becomes a kind of test. What was my deep inner reaction? Was I calm? Did I see the situation as a problem that requires some remedy? Or did anger well up? To what degree? Did I still feel in control, or did I lash out verbally and, perhaps, physically?

Suppose we "failed" the test, that is, we reacted with anger, either suppressed or overt. Then the episode becomes a lesson for us to ponder. Why did I lose patience? Where did I slip up? In what better way could I have approached this situation (and similar situations that may occur in the future)? If you subsequently raise these questions then you will have grasped the attitude of "Thank you; you're my teacher."

Afterword

This book began with questions: What is maturity? What do we mean when we say "He made a mature decision"? What is the relation between maturity and serenity? How do we attain to these conditions? The principal thesis of this book is that Buddhism and Yoga provide answers to these questions. Essentially, the teachings first reveal the pitfalls in ordinary, unreflective living. They then provide guidelines and practices for transforming ourselves and for progressing to a new mode of living. This transformation is accomplished by taming the cravings (passions, fears, agitations) and by challenging conditioned beliefs (attitudes, values, habits of thought). When transformed we are more than mature; we face the hurly-burly of the world with wisdom, hardiness, and confidence. Thus, these philosophies of Buddhism and Yoga are really applied psychologies. Earlier (p. 58) I mentioned the new contemporary movement toward positive psychology. Buddhism and Yoga are the quintessential positive psychologies. Indeed, they provide the intellectual framework for such a psychology.

The transformation that occurs after putting these teachings into practice also produces change at a deep level. We experience an inner peace, even when confronting the strongest challenges. Also, the essential self, the "you" (cf. Purusha, Buddha-nature) that exists beyond arbitrary conditioning and superficial conceptions, is revealed. It is for this reason, for this characterization of that deep, final realization, that these practical psychologies, with their emphasis on daily practices (meditations, asanas), are regarded as religions. Buddhism and Yoga begin with the practical and, after remarkable achievements in this realm, end with the spiritual.

At the outset I suggested that this book is a primer, an introduction to the most basic teachings of Buddhism and Yoga. It is introductory

213

in another sense. The discerning reader may have noticed a kind of paradox. On the one hand, the challenges that I described in daily life were all of the humblest occurrences, never life threatening. Typical examples included confronting someone smoking in a non-smoking area, a noisy neighbor, a problem with a spouse. On the other hand, the examples from the Eastern literature described challenges in the extreme. Monks confronted great pain (the monk in the torture chamber, p. 3), the threat of death (the monk caught between the tiger and the abyss, p. 99), or death itself (the monk's attitude toward the soldiers who kill him, p. 48).

My sense in presenting the teachings of Buddhism and Yoga was that the reader would be new to them, to their radical emphasis on self-transformation. The examples that I personally presented, therefore, were intended to illustrate the first steps on this new path. The Eastern examples illustrate the behavior at the far end of the path. This relationship between the Western and Eastern examples is nicely symbolized by a Yoga posture. The Yoga master may illustrate an extreme, rather contorted position. Those of us who are new to Yoga, however, begin with a first approximation. But we have the faith that perseverance will bring us closer to the final condition. This book, then, is also a primer in the behaviors it encourages you to change. The potential for radical change, however, is not ignored. The Buddhist and yogic examples show that the change in outlook can extend even to life and death.

To vividly emphasize this point, I include here one final tale. It is a follow-up to the story of the monk and the Samurai warrior (p. 174), where the monk, in order to teach the warrior the difference between heaven and hell, first insulted him.

> The warrior, after expressing his appreciation to the monk for the lesson he had so effectively conveyed, added: "You know, what you did was very risky. I could have run you through without blinking an eye." The monk replied, "I could be run through without blinking an eye. Can you meet that challenge?"

A secondary thesis of this book is that the outlook of Western psychology is congenial with that of Buddhism and Yoga. Both East and West see the human as caught in a causal matrix. Both see as their initial issue the suffering produced by those causal forces. Both seek and advocate empirically proven techniques that will not only alleviate that suffering but that will produce a mature happiness. It would obviously be of great value for the adherents of both systems, East and West, to be aware of each other. They can only benefit from each others insights and methods. It is hoped that this book will help to promote that awareness.

References

Annett, J. (1995). Imagery and motor processes. *British Journal of Psychology, 86,* 161–167.

Arnold, E. (1894). *The light of Asia.* Boston: T.Y. Crowell.

Axelrod, D. (1989). *Resurrections.* Merrick, NY: Cross-Cultural Communications

Bahm, A. J. (1961). *Yoga: Union with the ultimate.* New York: Ungar.

Bandura, A. (1986). *Social foundations of thought and action.* Englewood Cliffs, NJ: Prentice-Hall.

Beck, A. T. (1970). Cognitive therapy: Nature and relation to behavior therapy. *Behavior Therapy, 1,* 184–200.

Benson, H. (1975). *The relaxation response.* New York: William Morrow.

Benson, H. (1987). *Your maximum mind.* New York: Random House.

Berger, B. G., & Owen, D. R. (1992). Mood alteration with Yoga and swimming. *Perceptual and Motor Skills, 75,* 1331–1343.

Birch, B. B. (1995). *Power Yoga.* New York: Fireside.

Buber, M. (1937). *I and thou.* (R. G. Smith, Trans.). Edinburgh: Clark.

Carlson, R. (1997). *Don't sweat the small stuff.* New York: Hyperion.

Christensen, A. (1987). *The American Yoga association beginner's manual.* New York: Simon & Schuster.

Christoff, K. A., Scott. W. O. N., Kelley, M. L., Schlundt, D. D., Baer, G., & Kelly, J. A. (1985). Social skills and social problem-solving training for shy young adolescents. *Behavior Therapy, 16,* 468–477.

Csikszentmihalyi, M. (1990). *Flow: The psychology of optimal experience.* New York: Harper & Row.

Desikachar, T. K. V. (1977). *Religiousness in Yoga.* University Press of America.

D'Zurilla, T. J. (1986). *Problem-solving therapy.* New York: Springer.

Egoscue, P., & Gittines, R. (1998). *Pain free.* New York: Bantam.

Ellis, A. (1962). *Reason and emotion in psychotherapy.* New York: Lyle Stuart.

Ellis, A., & Harper, R. A. (1975). *A new guide to rational living.* Englewood Cliffs, NJ: Prentice-Hall.

Friedel, R. (1992). Perspiration in perspective: Changing perceptions of genius and expertise in American invention. In R. J. Weber & D. N. Perkins (Eds.), *Inventive minds,* pp.11–26. New York: Oxford.

Gethin, R. (1998). *The foundations of Buddhism.* New York: Oxford.

Herman, A. L. (1973). *The Bhagavad Gita.* Springfield, IL: Thomas.

Herodotus. (1942). *The Persian wars.* (G. Rawlinson, Trans.). New York: Modern Library.

Herrigal, E. (1953). *Zen in the art of archery.* (R.F.C. Hull, Trans.). New York: Pantheon.

Hittleman, R. L. (1969). *Yoga, Twentyeight-day exercise plan.* New York: Bantam.

Housman, A. E. (1927). *A shropshire lad.* London: Richards.

Jacobson, N. S. (1977). Training couples to solve their marital problems, Part I: Problem-solving skills. *International Journal of Family Counseling, 5,* 22–31.

Lange, A. J., & Jakubowski, P. (1976). *Responsible assertive behavior.* Champaign, IL: Research Press.

Levine, M. (1994). *Effective problem solving* (2nd ed.). Englewood Cliffs, NJ: Prentice-Hall.

Levine, M. (1997). *Look down from clouds.* Centereach, NY: Writers Ink Press.

Maslow, A. (1970). *Motivation and personality* (2nd ed.). New York: Harper & Row.

Masters, E. L. (1915). *Spoon river anthology.* New York: MacMillan.

Moffat, A. L. (1961). *Monghut the king of Siam.* Cornell, NY: Cornell University Press.

Nelson, T. O. (1992). *Metacognition.* Needham Heights, MA: Allyn & Bacon.

Novaco, R. W. (1975). *Anger control.* Lexington, MA: Heath

O'Connell, D. F., & Alexander, C. N. (1994). Introduction. In D. F. O'Connell & C. N. Alexander (Eds.), *Self-recovery,* (pp. 1–10). Binghamton, NY: Haworth.

Ornish, D. (1990). *Dr. Dean Ornish's program for reversing heart disease.* New York: Ballentine.

Peck, S. M. (1978). *The road less traveled.* New York: Simon & Schuster.

Rahula, W. (1974). *What the Buddha taught* (2nd ed.). New York: Grove Press.

Rakos, R. F. (1991). *Assertive behavior.* London: Routledge.

Rogers, C. R. (1961). *On becoming a person.* Boston: Houghton Mifflin.

Skinner, B. F. (1965). *Science and human behavior.* New York: The Free Press.

Seligman, M. E. P. (1991). *Learned optimism.* New York: Knopf.

Seligman, M. E. P. (1999). The President's Address. *American Psychologist, 54,* 559–562.

Smith, P. W., Compton, W. C., & West, W. B. (1995). Meditation as an adjunct to a happiness enhancement program. *Journal of Clinical Psychology, 51,* 269–273.

Sternbach, R. A. (1966). *Principles of psychophysiology.* New York: Academic Press.

Thich Nhat Hanh. (1991). *Old path white clouds.* Berkeley, CA: Parallax.

Zimbardo, P. G. & Gerrig, R. J. (1999). *Psychology and life, 15th ed.* New York: Longman.

Additional Readings

BUDDHISM

Arnold, E., (1894). *The light of asia*. Boston: T. Y. Crowell. *Primarily a beautiful poetic rendering of the life of the Buddha.*

Rahula, W. (1974). *What the Buddha taught* (2nd ed.). New York: Grove Press. *An excellent next step for readers of my book. Rahula is a monk from Sri Lanka who presents the basics of Theravada Buddhism. The second edition also includes some important original sources.*

Gethin, R. (1998). *The Foundations of Buddhism*. New York: Oxford. *A good follow-up to Rahula. Gethin describes the various Buddhist movements, from Theravada to Zen, along with many of the issues of modern Buddhism.*

Thich Nhat Hanh. (1991). *Old path white clouds*. Berkeley, CA: Parallax Press. *The life of the Buddha, and of a community of monks, as well as some of the teachings, all told as delightful stories.*

Goddard, D. (Ed.) (1938). *A Buddhist bible*. Boston: Beacon Press. *A selection of readings from the various Buddhist groups. This and the next book are for those who wish to start reading original sources.*

Walshe, M. (Trans.) (1995). *The long discourses of the Buddha*. Somerville, MA: Wisdom Publications. *One of the basic collection of sources central to Theravada Buddhism.*

YOGA

Bahm, A. J. (Trans.). (1961). *Yoga, union with the ultimate*. New York: Ungar. *The teachings of Patanjali, with commentary. Patanjali systemized Yogic ideas thousands of years ago in an outline form. Bahm's comments help clarify the teaching.*

Birch, B. B. (1995). *Power Yoga*. New York: Fireside. *A comprehensive treatment of the effects of yoga practice. Many advanced asanas are included.*

Christensen, A. (1987). *The American Yoga association beginner's manual*. New York: Simon and Schuster. *Asanas for beginning practitioners. Breathing, diet, and philosophy are also described.*

Desikachar, T. K. V. (1977). *Religiousness in Yoga*. University Press of America. *Based upon lectures given by Desikachar at Colgate University. It clearly communicates to a western audience the wide range of yogic teaching.*

Herman, A. L. (Trans.). (1973). *The Bhagavad Gita*. Springfield, IL: Thomas. *One of the classic sources of yogic teaching. The God, Krishna, teaches the warrior, Arjuna, the essentials of yogic wisdom.*

Hittleman, R. (1969). *Guide to Yoga Meditation*. New York: Bantam. *An introduction to meditation practice as well as to the theory of Yoga.*

Author Index

221

Subject Index

(Note: Foreign terms are given in Bold, with a brief definition)